Skyline
2019

Cyberworld Publishing

www.cyberworldpublishing.com

Skyline
2019

*An Anthology of
Prose and Poetry by
Central Virginia Writers*

Olivia Stowe, ed.

Table of Contents

Poetry

Prose Nonfiction

About the Authors

Introduction

Skyline 2019, the sixth in a series of annual publisher's anthologies produced by Cyberworld Publishing, showcases the prose and poetry talents of writers who live or work in Central Virginia or otherwise have writing connections to the region. The title of the anthology is taken from the Skyline Drive, the parkway skipping along the top of the Blue Ridge Mountains in Virginia and providing centering for the region to which the authors showcased here are connected. The first four editions followed the seasons in cover image and *Skyline* contest themes. The theme for the fifth edition and 2017's annual *Skyline* writing contest, was "nighttime on the mountain." This edition's contest theme is "winter holidays."

Other than the 2019 *Skyline* contest theme, there is no set theme for the other short stories, poems, and essays in this anthology, the content of which also includes pieces by the judges, editors, and publisher of *Skyline*, and selected award-winning pieces in regional contests in 2018 and 2019. Each of these works can be discovered and appreciated on its own context and merits. As with earlier *Skyline* editions, eclecticism is the hallmark word for this collection. A third of the works found here won or placed in various Virginia regional and statewide writing contests in 2018 and 2019. The foundation for the juried contest selections combine the 2019 *Skyline* writing contest and selected placers in the 2018 and 2019 contest of the Blue Ridge Writers (BRW) club. Selected contest-placing works from the 2019 poetry awards of the Poetry Society of Virginia; a second-placed poem in the 2019 Writer's Eye contest, sponsored by the Fralin Museum of the University of Virginia; and a 2018 Jefferson Madison Regional Library/WriterHouse prize-winning poem are published here as well.

Also included in the anthology are works by the *Skyline* winter holidays contest poetry judge, award-winning poet David Black, and the contest nonfiction judge, Stephen Bush (the *Skyline* publisher), as well as by volume editor, Olivia Stowe, and executive *Skyline* editor Gary D. Kessler. Novelist Sarah Collins Honenberger judged the fiction for the *Skyline* winter holidays contest, as she has done for all previous editions of *Skyline*. As always, we are grateful to our judges for their dedicated work in these contests.

The anthology is made up of thirty-seven works by twelve authors, presented in three sections: fiction (ten short stories), poetry (nineteen poems), and nonfiction (seven essays). Half of the authors here are represented by more than one work and, most of them, in varied media to showcase their writing skills.

Each edition of *Skyline* has lifted a featured writer or poet for recognition in addition to the works of invited established authors and contest judges. This edition, of course, celebrates Erin Newton Wells, who excels in all categories of writing featured by *Skyline*. Erin is truly a gifted writer, and without her large volume of award-winning work during this period of *Skyline* coverage, this edition would not have been possible.

A notable additional section to this anthology is the "About the Authors" section, which provides fascinating, I think, literary background notes on the authors connected with the Central Virginia region and represented in this collection. Many of these authors have been consistently presented in *Skyline* over its six years of existence.

As with the five earlier annual *Skyline* editions, it has been a delight to work with and discovering the many varied themes, writing approaches, and high quality of writing of these Central Virginia writers. I hope you will find these works as fresh and as entertaining and thought provoking as I have. These indeed are exceptional writers who deserve to have their works highlighted and represented in the marketplace.

Olivia Stowe
Volume Editor
Skyline 2019

PROSE FICTION

A Visit from Grandfather Frost

P. A. Duncan

(First place, fiction, *Skyline* Winter Holidays Contest, 2019)

Bukharin-Fisher Residence
Geneva, Switzerland
January 6, 2018

The turning of a doorknob from a room down the hall pulled Mai Fisher from much-desired sleep. Being head of a global espionage organization meant long days and occasional sleepless nights, but she'd promised her family this first Christmas in their new country, she'd be home.

The patter of small feet in the hallway and down the stairs brought her fully awake. She sighed. Ivan was up again. Since the Christmas tree had gone up a week ago, he'd gotten up in the middle of the night, every night, to go wait, he explained, for *"Ded Moroz."*

Grandfather Frost. The Russian version of Santa Claus.

She muffled her groan in her pillow. She'd set the alarm for 0400 so she and Alexei could put presents beneath that tree to perpetuate the myth of not only *Ded Moroz* but Santa Claus. At just after two in the morning, Ivan might stay awake, and there'd be no need for the pretense. She and Alexei had always had their differences, and this was a new one. She didn't want to lie to the child about Christmas, and Alexei wanted to continue what the child's real grandmother had started. Mai's reticence, he'd decided, was because she hadn't accepted the boy as their son.

* * * *

A Week Earlier

13

As he settled onto his side of the bed, Alexei Bukharin said, "Have you made arrangements to be home for Orthodox Christmas?"

"Yes. Quigg and I are going to swap. I'll be on site tomorrow, regular Christmas Day, and he'll be there for Orthodox Christmas."

Mai Fisher burrowed under her covers and closed her eyes.

"I confess," Alexei said, "I'm excited to see Ivan's face on Christmas Day. All he can talk about is being good so Grandfather Frost will bring him presents."

"He's always good," Mai murmured, "without a myth inducing it."

"It's not a myth to children."

"No, it's an enormous lie adults tell children to elicit a few days of good behavior. I hate lying to him."

"It's a harmless lie that gives him joy."

Mai sighed. She wasn't going to get to sleep after all. She turned over until she faced Alexei. "I hated all the lying we did to Natalia," she said, "for years and years until she figured it out and pushed back."

"That was different. Hiding the reality of our being spies was a safety and security concern. It's not the same as allowing a child who lost his only relative six months ago to continue to believe in Grandfather Frost."

"Either Alex Jr. or Barrett E. will likely spill the beans anyway," Mai said of Natalia's twin sons. "They informed me yesterday there wasn't a Santa Claus because it was a physical impossibility for him to go to every house in the world in twenty-four hours. A wonderful piece of reasoning, but they said they wouldn't tell Rachael M. and Ivan. I was tempted to let them."

"Mai, this is important to Ivan. Let's not add another trauma on top of the other."

"God, Alexei, learning there's no Santa Claus isn't a trauma."

"It could be for him." Alexei rolled onto his back, eyes on the ceiling. "This attitude of yours isn't surprising. You consider him an unwanted distraction."

"I do not!"

"You still won't warm up to him."

Mai raised up on one elbow. "Where the hell are you getting this?"

"You tolerate him, Mai. That's the extent of your emotions toward him."

"And you're bloody close to sleeping in another room. Ivan is not a distraction to me. You and I were on the verge of being empty nesters again, and he came along to make us a family once more. Something we needed or we'd have easily slipped into our own separate worlds."

She, too, flopped on her back, the gulf of the large bed between them. She hated arguing in bed. There were much more pleasant things to do there, but Alexei always seemed to bring up hot topics at bedtime, and not the hotness she found desirable.

"I hate having to pretend there's a Santa Claus. Or a Grandfather Frost," she murmured. "It's stuff and nonsense. Dishonest stuff and nonsense."

"He drew those pictures for you today and—"

"And I gushed over both of them, Alexei. They were adorable, and it was sweet, and I think they're precious."

Ivan had drawn his version of their holiday tree, with a tall man standing next to it. Popi, Ivan had explained. Though Alexei was tall, he wasn't as tall as the eight-foot tree, except perhaps in Ivan's six-year-old eyes. He'd drawn Mai as well, dressed all in black as she often was, and had used a bright red crayon for her hair. Between them, holding their hands, was Ivan himself. He'd labeled each one of them: Попи (Popi), Мама (that looked the same in Russian or English), and Иван (Ivan). The other picture was of Grandfather Frost. He looked like the usual Santa Claus only by virtue of the long, white beard, but Grandfather Frost was a resident of Siberia. He wore blue breeches and tunic, a long blue crystal-embroidered, fur-trimmed brocade coat, and a blue, fur hat with two curving horns that met above his head. He carried a staff of ice and a blue sack full of gifts.

The drawings were adorable, they were sweet, and she did think they were precious.

"You don't love him," Alexei said, after a pause long enough she'd almost fallen asleep.

She turned her back to him. "Keep this up, and I'll doubt I love you," she muttered.

The mattress shifted as he turned, too, and moved closer. "Mai, he needs to see he's loved, and he needs to see that from you."

"Alexei, you know I've never been effusive with children. It's not me to gush all over him that he's loved. He is."

"I'm not sure he knows that."

"I see what this is."

"All right. I'll bite. What is this?"

"You're having second doubts about being a father at seventy-four—not the only one in the world, I'm sure—and you're transferring your doubt to me."

His sigh was warm against her neck. "Ah, I see we've had one too many sessions with shrinks."

"Alexei, I've had the same doubts. Having Alex Jr., Barrett, and Rachael around is one thing. We can give them back to their parents when we're pooped. We can't do that with Ivan."

"Ah, ah, don't say we're stuck with him."

"I was *not* going to say that."

"There was no way I was leaving him for a Russian state orphanage."

"We've already had that discussion, and I agree with your decision. He's here. He's our son, and we'll give him the best life we can."

"Including Grandfather Frost?"

"What answer will let me get some sleep tonight, Old Man?"

He spooned against her back. "You were singing a different tune about this old man last night."

"Well, he wasn't accusing me of not loving our child then." She reached behind her and found something interesting. "Will that get me some sleep?"

He moved his hips away from her. "Go to sleep. We'll save that up for another time."

* * * *

Mai listened for the sounds of Ivan coming back upstairs. No such luck. She turned her head to see Alexei hadn't stirred. Or he was pretending he hadn't heard the child. Another sigh, and she rose from bed and tiptoed downstairs in her yoga pants and long-sleeved tee-shirt. She found Ivan where she expected to find him, in the family room, sitting on the floor, staring up at the Yule tree with its twinkling white lights.

She had to admit the scene was right out of a sappy Christmas card, the child sitting there in his Christmas-themed one-piece pajamas, gazing at the tree, the soft light dancing over his features. It stirred emotions in her she thought she'd buried with each of her failed pregnancies.

Mai stood beside him, and he looked up at her and smiled. That face, so innocent and trusting. She was glad he didn't look like his father, whom Mai had bested back when she was a spy. Ivan's biological father had been a poor excuse for a human being, but Ivan looked nothing like him. Mai doubted she could have warmed to Ivan had he resembled his father. Ivan's dark hair and eyes, like his grandmother's, made him resemble Mai, if nothing else. He had a broad forehead and those killer cheekbones like Alexei's. Somehow, it seemed, he was destined to be their child.

"Mama," Ivan said. He'd called her that almost from the moment he'd seen her, and she hadn't put a stop to it. Natalia had called her Mums, but no child had ever called her Mama, until now. "Is not the tree beautiful?"

Alexei had worked on Ivan's English constantly for the past six months so Ivan could go to school after the holidays, but Ivan hadn't quite grasped the concept of contractions.

"It's indeed beautiful, but you should be in bed," Mai said. She cringed inwardly as she spoke the next words. "Grandfather Frost won't come if you're awake."

"I thought he maybe comes early, so I want to check. But I like the tree and the lights and to watch them." He looked at the tree and back up at Mai, tears now in his eyes. "I miss Baba," he said, his voice so small she had to strain to hear.

Well, shite, she thought. Though her knees and back would admonish her later, she sat on the floor beside him, and he crawled into her lap, clutching the teddy bear Alexei had given him when he'd rescued Ivan.

"Baba" had been Ivan's grandmother, a former Russian spymaster whose death had precipitated his rescue from Russia. Ivan had mentioned her a great deal in the first weeks after her death but hadn't for several months.

Leave it to the holidays to bring up things best forgotten, she thought.

"You haven't talked about Baba for a while," Mai said, smoothing his soft hair. "Does Christmas make you think of her?" He nodded, his head bobbing beneath her chin.

"We would have tree. Not as big as this, and it was all pink with silver balls and colored lights," he said.

Gad, Mai thought. She hadn't believed Valeriya Alekseevna to be tacky, but sometimes tacky appealed to a child.

"She would tell me Christmas story," Ivan murmured. He looked up at her again. "Can you tell Christmas story?"

"What story?" Mai asked. Please, she thought, don't let it be the Bethlehem-Jesus-in-a-manger story.

"The one about *babushka*."

His *babushka*? Oh, wait, there was that story Alexei used to tell Natalia at Christmas.

"Do you mean the story about Babushka and the three wise men?" Mai said.

Ivan nodded.

Bloody hell, she hadn't heard that story in years, not since Natalia was twelve or so. And, in fact, it wasn't even a Russian story. Alexei had found it somewhere and told it to Natalia the first Christmas after she'd come to live with them. He'd decided even though an American had written it, it was a very Russian story.

"I'll try to remember it," Mai said, "but you may have to help me."

He gazed at her, again with the face of innocence, love shining in his eyes. She was way too old to be this child's mother. Alexei lamented the same thing about being his father. How could they be a family long enough for Ivan to become a man?

"Let's see if I can remember how it goes," Mai said. "In a small Russian village lived a woman named Babushka. She liked to keep her house tidy and clean, always sweeping, dusting, polishing. People in the village thought she had the most beautiful house and garden."

"And her cooking was best," Ivan said. "Like Popi's."

"Yes, his cooking is wonderful, isn't it? One night all the villagers were talking about a new star that had appeared in the sky, but she was too busy with her cleaning to look. She said, 'Such a fuss about star. There are uncountable stars. What's one more?'"

Mai used a thick Russian accent for Babushka, and Ivan giggled.

Mai continued, "The villagers tried to get her to look, but she said, 'I'm behind in my work, so behind I'll have to work all night,' and she set to cleaning her house. She could hear the sounds of celebration about the star, but she ignored them and kept up her cleaning until it was almost dawn."

"Then, three men did loud knocking at door," Ivan said.

"Not simply three men but three kings, from faraway countries. I think Babushka was annoyed they had interrupted her cleaning," Mai said, "but she was polite when she answered the door. What did they say to her?"

"Villagers say your house is best in village," said Ivan, "and we will stay here."

Mai had to stifle her laughter at the serious, demanding tone Ivan had taken. "Babushka couldn't understand why they wanted to stay at her house, but the village had a reputation to uphold."

"What is re-put-a-shun?" Ivan asked.

"The village always welcomed travelers passing through, gave them food, places to stay," Mai said, improvising. "It was known all over the world as a safe place for travelers, even when they were strangers. So, Babushka couldn't hurt the village's reputation. She let the men inside. The kings were amazed at Babushka's beautiful house, with all the pies and breads she had made. She had the kings sit at her table, and she served them all her best foods. 'Have you come a long way?' she asked them."

"And one king said, 'We have come from far away.' Oh, his name was Caspar. He was Caspar the king, not Casper, ghost who is friendly."

Again, Mai bit back her laugh. He was so serious in making sure she understood that. "That's right. And the one named Melchior said, 'We are following the new star.'"

"That new star again, Babushka thought. Why pay so much attention to that when there is work to do? 'Where will the new star lead you?' she asked. 'We don't know,' they said, 'but we believe it leads to a newborn king.'"

"I think they meant baby Jesus," Ivan said.

Now they were moving into uncomfortable territory, but having a debate about theism with a six-year-old was definitely not kosher. No pun intended, Mai thought.

"Indeed, they did," she said, "and they asked Babushka if she'd like to come with them and bring the baby king a gift like they were."

"What presents were they bringing?" Ivan asked.

He'd probably understand gold, but not frankincense and myrrh. "Gold, rare spices, and wonderful perfumes."

"Not toys?"

"This was a long time ago, and there were few toys. However, Babushka did have some toys. Long ago, she'd had a son, but he'd died. She'd kept all his toys in a cupboard. Thinking of her son made her sad. Like you when you thought of your Baba. But Babushka went back to her cleaning, of course. As she worked, the third king, Balthasar, said, 'What we hear of this new king is that he is the king for all. I'm sure he would welcome you, and I saw the toys you have in the cabinet. What a wonderful present they would be. When the star reappears tonight, come with us.' Babushka wasn't sure. The toys were all she had left of her son, and sometimes she looked at them to make sure she remembered him. She promised the kings she'd think about it."

Ivan sighed and said, "I had picture of Baba when she was young and pretty. Before she was sick. I could not bring it with me." Tears leaked from his sad eyes, and Mai used her sleeve to dry them.

"Do you want me to stop the story?" she asked.

He shook his head. "I want to hear it," he said.

"All right. Well, Babushka worked all day to straighten her house while the kings slept, and she wondered and wondered if she should go with them. She worried she didn't have decent clothes to wear for a new king. She worried no one would take care of her house while she was gone. She worried so much, she was surprised when it was night again. She told the kings she'd follow in a day and after she found a gift. They were disappointed, but they wished her well and left. Babushka went to the cupboard with all her son's toys. They'd been in there a long time and were dusty and dirty. Babushka couldn't give them to the new king like this, so she cleaned and cleaned until each toy was bright and shiny again. However, she was so tired she fell asleep, and when she woke she realized the kings were far ahead of her. She put on her best cloak, put the toys in a basket, and went after the kings."

"Did she find them?" Ivan asked.

"She didn't, but she went from village to village, always asking about them. Finally, she reached a big city with a palace, and she asked a guard if he'd seen the three kings and if he knew about the new baby king they'd come to see. Babushka was sad to learn not only had the kings left a few days before to return to their countries, but the new baby-king had as well. His birth upset the ruler of the city, and the baby king had to leave."

"Like I had to leave Russia?"

"Not exactly. No one was upset by your birth, but because your Baba was sick, she arranged for you to come live with us."

Ivan nodded again. "Are you glad I come to live with you?"

"Very glad," Mai said.

Ivan's eyelids drooped a bit. "Can you finish story, Mama?"

"Babushka was upset she didn't get to see the baby king, and the story says she wanders from village to village with her basket of toys, looking for the baby king still, that she loved him and wanted him to have the toys so much she was going to find him, even if it took forever. But you're right here, and Popi and I don't have to look any further than your room."

The sigh he gave was one of contentment, followed by a long yawn, and Mai held him until he was asleep. She heard a whisper of movement from behind her and looked over her shoulder. Alexei came from the darkness into the room.

"You got it mostly right," he murmured, with a smile.

"Good. I made most of it up on the spot."

"He liked it. That's all that matters."

"Can you take him back up to bed? I have to make a phone call."

"Now? I thought you left your deputy in charge so you could spend time with your family."

Honestly, sometimes she wondered how they'd managed to stay together forty years.

"I did. A check-in. No more than five minutes," she said.

He bent down and picked up the boy, cradling him in his arms. "Five minutes. No more." He winked at her. "I'll be waiting."

When she was sure Alexei was upstairs, Mai let herself into her secure home office, made a call, gave explicit instructions, hung up, and went back to bed.

* * * *

Bukharin-Fisher Residence
Orthodox Christmas Day

Alexei decided if his wife looked at her work phone one more time, he was going to take it from her. He smiled. The fact she'd put up a fight was a tad arousing.

His immediate family was around him, and he felt a certain contentment, a fullness of heart he'd seldom had in his work. His granddaughter, Natalia, and her husband, Alex, sorted the prodigious amount of toys each of their children had received. The twins, Alex Jr. and Barrett E., had claimed the kitchen counter to assemble some enormous Lego kit, but at least they were quiet under their seventeen-year-old uncle Sergei's supervision. Alexei's son Peter and Peter's wife, Bridget, sat off by themselves talking in quiet tones. Alexei hadn't seen his son this happy in a long time. Ivan and Rachael M. were using the hallway as a track for the three-wheeled scooters they'd both gotten from Grandfather Frost.

And Mai checked her phone again. An admonition on his lips, Alexei stopped when he saw her expression, one of relief, tinged with happiness.

What was that, he wondered. An op she was worried about? An agent out of touch who was found?

He was about to ask her when Natalia reminded him it was time to put out the Christmas Day meal: roast pork and roast goose, meat dumplings, vegetable salads, several different fruit pies, and the *kozulka*, Christmas cookies in the shape of a goat, deer, or sheep. Ivan had picked the deer, "like Rudolf with red nose," he'd said. Alexei had made certain each one had a dot of red frosting for a nose.

In the midst of arranging the buffet and setting the table, the doorbell rang, and Alexei frowned. If that was someone from Mai's office . . .

"I'll get it," Mai said and rushed for the front door.

Alexei's scowl deepened.

"What?" Natalia said to him. "You're all frowny."

"Today was supposed to be family time. No work," he said.

"Ease up, Pops. You know someone wouldn't have come from the office until it was earth-shattering."

"Exactly what I'm afraid of."

Mai wasn't at the door long. She returned to the family room, where Rachael M. and Ivan had put the scooters aside to read through the books they'd received. Rachael M. helped Ivan with his pronunciation of some of the words.

"Who was at the door?" Alexei said. His tone must have betrayed his displeasure because Mai looked at him and raised an eyebrow.

"Ivan?" she said. "That was an assistant from Grandfather Frost. He forgot to leave one of your presents." Mai held a small package wrapped in shiny red paper and garnished with a gold ribbon.

"Another present for me?" Ivan asked and came to her.

Mai gave it to him, and he carefully tore the paper away. Rachael M. came to look over his shoulder. He pried open the box and gave a squeal, not of fear or anger or disappointment but of such utter delight it rendered Alexei motionless.

Ivan babbled excitedly in Russian and ran to Alexei. "Look, Popi, look! It is Baba! A picture of Baba!"

Alexei looked at what the boy held in his hands. A simple wooden frame holding what had to have been a surveillance photo of Alekseevna taken a few years ago, but it was a face-on shot, candid, as if she were unaware of the scrutiny. Ivan placed kiss after kiss on the glass.

But how . . . Oh. The overnight phone call. Mai had had someone from The Directorate pull up a photo of former FSB Director Valeriya Alekseevna from a dossier somewhere, had it printed, had it framed, had it wrapped, and had it brought here.

Alexei looked at Mai, the woman he'd loved for a long time. Her smile was secretive, as befitted who she was, and when she looked at Ivan in his joy, it was with love.

Lull Them into a Sense of Complacency

P. A. Duncan

("Lull Them into a Sense of Complacency" is a short story from an as-yet unpublished collection of espionage short fiction entitled, *The Moscow Rules*. The title is "Moscow Rule Number Seven.")

Paris, France
Present Day

"I am telling you, Yuri, we are wasting our time," Fyodor said.

"We are in Paris at Christmastime, watching a pretty girl, Fedya. What is wasting time with that?" Yuri asked.

"She is a dead end. For three weeks now, we have watched her leave her flat, go to the embassy, leave the embassy at the end of the day, go to her flat. Oh, but there are the occasions she eats at a restaurant with friends or goes Christmas shopping or does the marketing, but it has been the same. Every day. For three weeks."

"I still do not see what there is to complain about. We are on expense account in Paris, and I am planning on buying my wife some French lingerie for Christmas. This duty is not as bad as some. Feel sorry for our poor comrades who are spying on the American president."

"True. But a few more days and I think we can safely conclude that this woman is exactly what she says she is: merely a secretary at the embassy."

"Fedya, I will tell you a story about a mere secretary at an embassy. Back in the late seventies, I think it was, a woman was transferred from the U.S. State Department to a position in the U.S. Embassy in Moscow, as a secretary. That was back in the KGB days, of course, and it was my training officer who was assigned to watch her. She was always on time to work. Did some sightseeing. Took pictures but always of the public places, never

25

anything strategic, she never went anywhere she wasn't supposed to, so after a few weeks, he slacked off watching her."

"And the point of this fairy tale?" Fyodor asked.

"Let me finish . . . . Oh, wait. She has never gone into that coffee shop before."

"Perhaps she is to meet someone."

"Yes, Fedya. I feel like a cup of that fancy coffee holiday drink. The peppermint one with the candy cane. How about you?"

"Are you buying?"

"We are on expense account, Fedya. President Dmitri Kargin is buying."

Yuri and Fyodor bought their coffees, settled at a table among the gold and silver holiday decorations, and watched the woman. She sat at a window table, sipped her coffee, and read a French newspaper.

"Yura, do you think the way she is folding and refolding the paper is semaphore?"

"You mean, is she signaling someone? I don't know." Yuri set his phone on the table, the video recorder on to capture her movements.

"It would be good if after all these dull days something exciting would happen, yes?" Fedya said.

"Do not be so eager for excitement. Now, I was telling you about this American secretary in Moscow. So, they stopped following her. Come to find out, she had been filling and clearing dead drops in Moscow for a KGB man who was selling secrets to the CIA. They caught her one night filling a drop—in a hollow brick placed in a bridge abutment. She started screaming like a demon, hoping to alert her mole to run away. And, *boizhe moi*, she put up a fight. It turns out her husband had been an intelligence officer in Vietnam and was killed. She blamed the KGB for that, so she joined the CIA to avenge him. She learned all these martial arts, you see, and she gave the agents trying to capture her a good thrashing. One agent said he could not fuck for a year afterward because she'd kicked him so hard in the balls."

"Did they capture her?"

"Eventually and after many bruised balls and shins. When they interrogated her, she stuck to her story. Even when they showed her the hollow brick she had put in place for her mole.

26

She kept saying I am so-and-so, and I am a secretary at the American embassy. You have no right to detain me. On and on. Over and over."

"What happened to her mole?"

"He ignored her screaming and tried to clear the drop anyway. We caught him. Brought him to the Lubyanka. Removed everything from his pockets. You know, standard procedure. Damnedest thing happened. At his request, she'd given him a pen with a poison capsule. It was a simple enough looking pen. No one thought to examine it. When he went to sign his confession, he said the pen we gave him didn't work. So, we gave him the pen from his pocket. He was too fast. He broke the pen open, got the capsule out, and swallowed it. Almost killed two doctors when they cut him open for the autopsy." Yuri shook his head.

"And the woman?"

"We kept her for a while. Roughed her up a bit. You know what I mean."

"You mean . . ."

"Gang rape to convince her she was in the wrong business. A few weeks later, we exchanged her for an illegal of ours the CIA rolled up."

"Kept her out of the business, then, eh?" Fedya asked.

"No. I hear she went on to be some big deal at the CIA. So, I am saying it is possible this pretty young woman is not merely a secretary. I mean, her name. Cybill Fleming. Please, it is the Americans trying to be subtle."

"What do you mean, Yura?"

"Remember KAL007?"

"The airliner the military shot down in, what, eighty-four, eighty-five?"

"Nineteen eighty-three. On a routine flight from Anchorage to Seoul, but it strayed into our prohibited airspace. The military in the east thought it was a spy plane and shot it down, killing everyone on board, including, I think, a congressman from America. All very sad, and I do not want to think about what happened to that military commander. But . . . I always thought the Americans would try to fool us."

"I am not following you, Yura."

"That flight had never been designated 007 before, and the Americans always thought we were stupid. 'Let us designate the flight after a fictional spy. Those stupid Russians will not get it.'"

"I see. So, it *was* a spy plane."

Yuri shrugged. "I think so."

"So, you are saying the Americans would give her a name like Cybill Fleming, after the man who wrote all those silly James Bond books, because they think we would not figure it out?"

"Exactly. And Fleming's books—Ian Fleming, that is—were not silly. He, of course, had been a spy. It is the movies that are silly and awful. Ah, do not look, but she is getting up."

Yuri and Fyodor looked busy on their phones as the young woman they'd watched for three weeks walked past them toward the toilets. Fyodor, who faced the rear of the coffee shop, murmured, "She went into the ladies' room. Did she leave her paper at her seat, anything that might be a signal?"

Yuri, who faced the front of the cafe, said, "No. Nothing. She even threw away her trash and put her cup back on the coffee bar. She is probably preparing to leave. Finish your coffee so we can resume the hunt."

"The hunt for nothing."

"You know, Fedya, I am convinced you are right, but what do you say? Let us milk it for another week, all expenses paid. In Paris. At Christmas. What do you say?"

"Sounds good to me. Where should we plan on dinner tonight? Or should we—"

"Excuse me, gentlemen."

Yuri and Fyodor looked up. Two men in business suits and overcoats stood next to their table. One man flashed some identification.

"French police," the man said. "Come with us, please. Quietly. There is no need to make a scene."

Yuri sighed and said, "No, there is no need."

"But, Yuri . . ."

"Come, Fedya, no need to protest. She made us," Yuri said, standing. "We are not armed," he said to the policemen, if that's what they were. More likely DGSE—the General Directorate for External Security.

The woman appeared beside the two Frenchmen. She'd switched coats, covered her hair with a scarf, almost like a Muslim, and wore sunglasses large enough to obscure half her face.

To Yuri, she said, in good Russian, "Since you're so fond of history, make sure you tell your friend about the *Moskovskiye Pravila*. Number seven, particular." She gave them a dazzling smile, nodded to the Frenchmen, and left.

As the Frenchmen walked them to a car, Fyodor said, "What did she mean, *Moskovskiye Pravila*?"

"The Moscow Rules, developed long ago by the CIA for new operatives sent to Moscow. An informal system of protocols so what is happening to us right now did not happen to them."

"And number seven? What is that?"

"The seventh Moscow Rule. 'Lull them into a sense of complacency.'" Yuri sighed and said, "Damn, I was looking forward to seeing my wife in French lingerie. Ah, perhaps we'll be out by Valentine's Day. You know, Fedya, this Cybill Fleming, she reminds me of another woman operative. Not from the CIA. From the UN."

"You mean the one who married the traitor?"

"Yes. Her. Now, that is a long story, but I think I will probably have the time."

A Time of Coming Toward

Erin Newton Wells

(Second place, fiction, *Skyline* Winter Holidays Contest, 2019)

What is the sound outside? Leftover leaves scuttling in a gust of cold wind. It brings December. It blows the last month away.

No. It is a voice muttering on the porch, a rhythm, low and talking to itself.

Someone moves back and forth beyond the tilted blinds, the window closed to a winter day, glass between us. I keep to the side, out of view. Who is it?

A circle of candles is on the table, the twine wicks new and unlit. A straw angel keeps watch on the mantel. I have set her there just now, before the sound drew me to the window.

Warmth grows in the room, a sense of expectation as the season begins and I prepare for it. But this low empty rhythm reminds me of the vast region wrapping its cold around the house outside, around the street and town, as far away as I can think.

An evergreen wreath with no ribbons yet hangs on the other side of the door where I placed it this day. We must wait for ribbons. We must be patient.

The muttering again. A gray figure, pacing, shaking its head. Who is on my porch?

Latin, if you have the pleasure of roaming through it, will give little doors into words. Here in the season of Advent, a time of quiet waiting while the rest of the world seems crazy with holiday, I know it also as a season of measured movement. The first part, "ad," means "to or toward," and the last is from "venio," meaning "come."

Step by step we come to it, not all at once. We consider each movement and arrive soon enough. Be still. Watch and listen.

"I don't know, I don't know."

The sounds outside become words. I see a woman between thin stripes of the blinds, her hair blown wild by wind. She wears an ancient sweater and a skirt with frayed hem almost to the ground, all of it dim and gray in winter light. She paces and mutters, a mystery in a season of mysteries.

"Gonna be, gonna be, gonna be."

The words quicken and gallop, run together, like a song lyric you cannot quite discern, her voice muffled through the wall of a house preparing for the quiet turning of the year.

"Gonna be, gonna be," she says, then stops.

She turns her head toward the door. My eyes slide toward it, then back. She cannot see me yet.

"Nawwwww," she expels the word in a plume of breath, a small winter wind.

"Never gonna," she says, and shakes her head.

She resumes the pace, arms wrapped around her chest.

By now it must be eighteen degrees, and lower to come, the warning out. Wrap the pipes. Shroud the shrubs. Keep the animals in. Snow, perhaps.

"Never gonna, no way, never, no way," the rhythm hitching and lame.

And the jinx is up.

I slip from the window, but not soon enough. She finds me through the glass, and I am compelled to stay there while she faces me for a good long minute, squints, sighs, a frost cloud formed by the gust.

Again, she tilts her head toward the door. My eyes move toward it, then back, the two of us staring through a slender stripe of the universe.

In the waiting time of Advent, the month-long pause in the calendar when some of us grow still enough to hear our lives pulse in our ears, I think I hear the woman breathe, even through the glass and the walls. I put my hand on the knob of the door with its brief fan light at the top, its five elegant panes giving but a glimpse of gray sky.

The air inside the room is soft and temperate, a gentleness on the spines of old books, the small spinet, the collection of kept things on which I can run my hand and remember. A smooth porcelain cat. A wooden box with gold inset leaves of ivy.

Here in the foyer is the mat on which I stand, its colors garnet and amber, a pattern of arabesques and medallions. Here, nearby, is the chamber for cloaks, hats, boots, gloves and scarves with which to keep warm, a door to slide and secure them.

A basket of oranges has been delivered from another world where the season is nothing like here. I will lift it and place it in the dining room to scent the house. Oranges. They used to be a great treasure, a rare gift, a delight, before the world became surfeited with such goods. A bright tag is tied to the wicker to greet me and wish me good cheer.

And here she is. I open the door, and here is my stranger. Gray hair, gray clothing, gray weather. The skin of her feet is gray from cold in brief, soft shoes of a ballerina, the sides split and spilling her toes on the cold slab of the porch.

"Don't mean nothin'," she says. "Don't mean no trouble."

She looks at me, looks down, looks to the side where the pear tree seems burnt this time of year, the twig ends knobby and dormant.

"You're cold," I say, the obvious.

"Don't mean nothin'."

I wait for her to tell me, but she does not, her eyes at her feet, the poor sad toes, the slippers someone else once danced in, perhaps with more joy and nimbleness.

"Are you lost?"

"No'um."

The bus stop is two blocks away, the wind bitter. How did she get here?

"Is there something I can do?"

"I come to see you want to hire on."

"Pardon?"

"I do all that. The floor. The toilet. I scrub real good. Do some washin' up the clothes. Out here, the yard. I can do that."

She waves her hand at the bleak lawn, the huddled shrubs and beds, the frozen clumps.

"Well, there's not much for that right now, is there?" I say, and laugh.

"No'um, cold and all."

"Did you ask at the other houses?"

"None a them home."

True. Most are away at work in the day. A cleaning woman, dropped like a gift at my door. Do I need one, the little I have for her to do?

"Can you tell me someone else you worked for?"

"It was away a piece. And she died. Old. I was real good to her."

"Not here, then, in this town."

She nods.

"And after that?"

"Been on my own awhile since."

Just that slight sour odor. Where does she sleep? Where does she stay? What a fool I am, a fool. I cannot bear this cold, a warm fleece jacket around me, warm sturdy shoes. I cannot bear the sight of those cold feet in thin ruined dancing slippers, the swirl of leaves, the winter wind.

"Will you come in, then?"

A look of alarm darts into her eyes, as if she might bolt. She turns her head and barely moves her mouth so I will not hear or see the muttering.

"Gonna be, gonna be," a rapid whisper, pretending she clears her throat.

That strange rhythm, the beat of a heart that keeps her alive.

She seems to melt in the foyer, the warmth, the fragrance of oranges, eyes wary as she looks into the room, an unknown kingdom.

"Please. Sit."

I show her a soft chair, but she will not go near it.

"No'um, I can stand."

"In the kitchen, then. We can sit at the table."

I lead her there. Slowly, as if the room will break, she agrees to take the plain wooden chair and sit at the plain table, the plain clock ticking on the wall, the simple curtains hanging motionless and serenely over the sink, a frozen life unfolding in the warmth.

"Now for coffee. Something to eat?"

"No'um. I don't mean no trouble."

She looks at her lap.

"Well, I need something to eat. I definitely need coffee. Look at the time."

It is already after twelve, the clock ticking forward, coming toward, coming toward.

I start the pot, make the sandwiches, set out plates and cups, and all the while the rhythm whispers to shore her up, a bridge made of twigs and thread over chasm after chasm.

"When do you think you could start?" I ask.

I take a seat and pour coffee for each of us. She looks at me as though I have lost my mind. And, of course, I have.

"Ma'am, you mean to hire me on?"

"If this is what you want. I guess I could use the help."

She views the gleaming kitchen.

"You keep a nice place."

"I do like it clean."

I push the plate of sandwiches toward her. She has barely taken a bite.

"I get down on my knees, scrub a floor end to end," she says.

"That's the way to do it."

"You don't have no tree up yet."

"A tree? Oh, not yet. I wait till later."

We eat, the sounds bright and sharp in the ticking silence of the kitchen.

"I could start anytime."

"Good. Let me think. Mondays?"

"I could do that."

"If it suits, mid morning would be best for me."

"You be here?"

"In my office, yes."

"I don't make no trouble."

"Of course. A little light work to get started. Dust and vacuum. Tidy up the bathrooms. What a pleasure not to have to do it all."

"Yes'um."

She has finished the sandwich, refuses more.

"You have family?" I ask.

She shakes her head.

"No one?"

35

"No'um."

"Everyone has family somewhere. We all come from somewhere."

"Not no more."

The rhythm begins, the mouth pretending to swallow, the clock beating time. It drowns out whatever must be kept beneath. Stupid me. I triggered it.

I propose a weekly sum, and she agrees. I do not want to send her out into the cold. Where will she go? I hand her two oranges at the door. I want to open the closet and wrap her in all these clothes, these boots, shape a soft pod of warmth around her in which she can nestle against the wind.

How do I even know she will return?

I clear the kitchen, then take a box from the shelf and set up the small rough structure of the empty creche on a living room table. I will wait for them to arrive from their year's rest among the tissue and take their places one by one, according to the story. I will wait for the house made of wood and sticks to be filled and come alive once more.

It starts so simply, the scene so spare, so possible.

When Aline calls, I am done and watching from the kitchen window as ghost deer in their pale gray coats the color of winter bark stand at the back of the house. There will be snow tonight. They are hungry and eating dry leaves. Their bodies know to do this when there is no fresh grass. They adapt to what is given or withheld.

I tell her about the woman. At first there is silence on the phone.

"You know you're crazy," she says. "You know that, don't you?"

More silence.

"What do you know about her? Nothing, right? She could murder you. Steal you blind. Are you there?"

"Yes."

The guard deer sees me and turns its flank broadside to shield the others, its black eyes never moving from my face.

"What kind of references does she have? Could she give you any?"

I tell her about the old lady who died, some ways off from here.

"Sophie. Sheesh. I mean, Sophie. You better cancel out right now. I mean, right now. Call her up. Make an excuse. What's her name, anyway?"

And I realize I do not know. I never asked. She never told. And as for calling her? Well.

Aline sputters.

The deer snorts and stamps its front hoof. At the signal, the others run into the wood along the border in back, the evergreen cypress dark and full, a place to hide.

I move through the week, the weekend, doing my work, doing small things. I unwrap the shepherds and look at their faces, tired and worn, even the young one. I unwrap the sheep.

I edit a manuscript, then another. Snow has begun.

On Monday, at ten, she arrives.

When I ask, she tells me her name is Yvonne. She pronounces it Why-vonne, then tells me people just call her Vonne. There is no phone, no number to call. No address.

I show her the vacuum, the cleansers, the cloths and brushes, and she works.

I work in my office. A light snow continues, and the white light surrounds me at my desk, white pages spread before me, a lit screen smooth as ice. One window looks from the side of the house. Everything is softly covered, muffled, no sound.

The vacuum hums through the rooms. Then she is quiet as she cleans the baths. I hear her come from the one in the hall. I hear her go up the stairs to the other, and after awhile she comes down.

"Ma'am?"

She stands just outside the office door.

"I'm done now."

"Good," I say. "That's fine."

I smile. She waits.

"You want to come and see?"

She looks over her shoulder toward the hall.

"I'm sure you did a fine job."

Her mouth begins to move.

"Now, let's see," I say, and look at my watch. "Let's call it an early lunch."

She looks down.

"I don't mean no trouble."

"I know." I set the papers aside and stand and go to the kitchen.

"I put it all away, where you told."

The vacuum, the cleaning tools.

"That's fine. Thank you."

She watches from the hall as I heat soup and set out bread and cheese.

"You have time for lunch, don't you, Vonne?"

"Ma'am, I don't mean no trouble."

"Of course you don't. But everyone has to eat. Please come. Sit with me."

And she does, cautiously looking around the room because it might vanish. I will vanish. The table and food will vanish.

She hunches in the chair until I begin, and I urge her to start. But she covers her face with her hands.

"You don't send me away?"

"Vonne, why would I do that? You've done the job we agreed on."

She lowers her hands. The lips are moving as though popping the tiniest bubbles, barely a trace. She begins to eat the soup.

In the foyer, I pay her, and she tucks it into the pocket of her skirt.

She looks again into the room.

"You don't have no tree yet."

"No. A few more weeks, and then I will."

Only shepherds, angels, a circle of candles, one of them now burned a bit. This is how the season begins and proceeds.

The dance slippers look damp. How has she managed in snow? I slide open the closet door and find the pair of winter boots, too large for me.

"Try these," I say. "I think they will fit."

"Oh, no'um. I got the bunion. I can't put a hard shoe on it."

"But these have soft fur inside and plenty of room."

38

They are Jim's boots. He will not need them now.

"No'um. I can't do that."

I watch her leave in the pitiful shoes, the street filling up again since the plow came in the night. Falling snow makes an absence into which she disappears.

When Aline calls, I tell her how well Vonne has done. Aline tells me I have gone completely out of it, her words. I ask her about other things. But she comes back to this in disbelief, her voice reaching through the phone to shake sense into me.

Another Monday, and Vonne is here, right at ten. Snow comes off and on, the ground always covered now, the evergreens weighted with heavy loads, bare trees turned to brittle lace.

She works. I work. I offer her lunch. I try to ask of her life, gently, as though pushing aside a curtain of feathers, brushing them smooth. Just once, the third Monday as we eat a simple meal, she opens a small space where it is hidden.

"Oh, ma'am, you got no way to know."

And it is true, I have no idea. I have always lived in this envelope of love softened around me, clear windows to look out, walls that keep me, a little scene that empties and fills with the seasons.

She tells me just a fragment of her shattered life, things she cannot put a name to and is speechless when she tries to go on, her mouth muttering with the rhythm that blots out what she does not want to remember. The bruises, the scars, unthinkable things from the time she is a child.

I pay her. I put a bag packed with apples and rolls in her hands, a small cake. She does not look at it, looks down at the patterns on the rug, but she takes it.

I hand her a folded woolen scarf from the closet.

"Please," I say. "To put around you and over your head."

At last she takes it, so little against the chill air, nothing for the bare, mottled skin on her ankles and feet, and she leaves.

The weary couple has arrived from the long journey, and they wait by the empty crib. Animals crowd around them, donkey and cow. The small space grows warm with their heat, their low breathing, the sharp smell of fresh straw laid over a grimy stall where animals have slept and eaten.

No tree yet. It will come. After four candles are lit, four weeks, I will find a small tree and dress it with trinkets. I will tie a bright bow on the wreath. In the night, the time of waiting will end, as it always does, and I will awake once more to the changed day.

Two packages have come, then three, the hurry now to bring them, time growing short. The carriers do not even ring the bell, just leave them on the porch and run, the heavy trucks marking paths through the quiet street.

"You want me to put these for you?" she asks on the fourth Monday when she sees them inside the door. "You got no tree."

"You may put them here," I say.

I show her a place beside a chair, beside a small table with a lamp, a table with the carved wooden figure of a sleeping lion, the grain of the wood following the curve of its beautiful body, the swivel of shoulders and hips.

"You don't want to open and put them out?"

"No. Not yet."

She stacks them largest to smallest, one atop another, like a brown parcel tree. They come from people who love me. I can tell by the address on each. They will each contain a lovely surprise.

She stares at the little house, the small people and beasts in their poses, waiting.

She cleans. I rearrange words. She scrubs the kitchen floor, moves the chairs into the hall. I hear the faint slur and shush as the brush moves round and round and she kneels to it.

The tiles are dry by noon, and we sit together in the kitchen to have our lunch. The room now smells of lemons from the cleanser she used.

"Will you come next Monday, Vonne? Not to work."

"Ma'am?"

Monday is the eve of the day toward which we move so slowly. I tell her I will find a small tree, perhaps a young fir that grows in the field past the wood behind my house. I will put it in a clay pot, set it on a table, and deck it with things I have collected all my life.

"Will you come?" I ask. "Will you help?"

"Ma'am? Ma'am?"

She gets up, leaves the room, and I know she is crying. I can hear it.

When she returns, she sits and nods to me, yes.

"Good, then. Good. It's better this way."

At the door, she wraps the scarf around her and takes the bag I hand her.

Then I take it back and set it on a stand and open the closet.

"Please," I say. "For me. Try them," and I hand her the boots.

Her mouth is moving, quivering. But she removes a slipper and pushes her foot into the padded shaft of a boot. Then she tries the other. She folds the slippers into a pocket.

"There. Now this."

I hand her a blue winter coat with a hood, and she puts it on. Jim's coat. I give her the bag, and she holds it to her chest and leans into the freezing air.

All the way down the street until she turns the corner, and halfway down that street until she steps behind the falling snow, I watch Jim's blue coat, Jim's winter boots as they vanish.

I will prepare the spare room for a guest, fluff the pillows, spread the nice quilt with its intricate pieces, set fresh towels in the hall bath. We will deck the small tree. We will arrange the final figures. We will light all the candles.

A Christmas Story

Deborah Prum

(Third place, fiction, *Skyline* Winter Holidays Contest, 2019)

> *Come, they told me*
> *Pa rum pum pum pum*
> *Our newborn King to see*
> *Pa rum pum pum pum*

Andi detested "The Little Drummer Boy" song. All that "pa rum pum pumming" drove her crazy. The substitute choir director, Ms. Jones, chose Andi's son, Maclain, and another boy named Tim, to be drummers. Snare drums harnessed to their narrow eight-year-old shoulders, the boys stood at either end of the top row of the risers, twin bookends with panicked expressions. Ms. Jones had selected them purely on the basis of their height, not at all with regard to their prowess with drumsticks or their rhythmic sensibilities. Why hadn't Ms. Jones chosen one drummer? Preferably not Maclain. One kid *not* keeping the beat would have been far less noticeable than two kids not keeping the beat each in their own unique ways. Musical hell.

Two weeks before the performance, Ms. Jones had sent home a recording of the song. Maclain listened to it hours on end. As he played along, he frequently dropped the drumsticks, which meant he'd have to go back to the beginning. Several nights, Andi had drifted off to sleep with the earworm *"Pa rum pum pum pum"* relentlessly thrumming through her brain.

Andi looked around, wondering if other parents secretly hated the drummer boy song, too. Not too many smiles. The audience still seemed on edge, not quite having recovered from the first song the choir had performed. During "Dreidel, Dreidel, Dreidel," a boy named Manuel projectile vomited from the top row of the risers, over and down to the front row, hitting several girls, three of whom ran screaming out of the room.

Mrs. Murphy, the choir director, was out having a hip replaced. She would have known never to place Manuel in the back row, regardless of his looming height. Even as a newcomer in Charlottesville, Andi had heard stories about "Manuel, the Anxiety Hurler." You could count on Manuel to throw up at athletic competitions, on SOL test days, field trips, and performances. He couldn't help it and was never fazed by the ruckus he caused. In fact, Manuel seemed to enjoy his notoriety, in a macho way.

Andi knew if Maclain ever threw up on stage, he'd be devastated. The event would spin into a weeklong depression. He would hole up in his room under the covers. Maclain always seemed desperate to fit in and blend in. Andi worried that he lacked confidence, that he seemed to be more of a follower than a leader. Had baby Eileen's death two years before damaged his sense of security? It had definitely damaged Andi's sense of security. Tears welled up.

The morning Eileen died, Andi had been running late. She'd rushed out the door, trying to get Maclain to school before the eight o'clock bell. Jacob was supposed to wake up and feed the infant. When she returned to their tiny house, a police car, fire truck, and ambulance blocked her way. She'd always remember a street full of lights, blinking red and blue. By the time she made it to her front steps, the EMTs were rushing out the door with Eileen, her two-month-old infant, purple and motionless, on the gurney. Her heart had already stopped. No one could ever say exactly why.

A sob rose up in her. Hold it together. You're at your son's Christmas concert. She took in a deep breath. Focus on the present.

She turned her attention to the choir, which dutifully plodded to the end of "The Little Drummer Boy." In theory, Mac and Tim were to finish the song with a flourish, a spectacular drumming duet. Maclain had practiced the grand finale endlessly, with varying results.

Andi didn't care whether Maclain performed well. She didn't push him to get straight As or hope he'd be a star basketball player. She loved him no matter what he could or couldn't do. Just plain average was good enough. Great, in fact. After Eileen died, something shifted. All that mattered to Andi was that Maclain was healthy and safe.

After Maclain's birth, she'd experienced years of miscarriages. Out of the blue came Eileen, a miracle, but a short-lived miracle, two months and gone. Andi sighed. All she knew for sure was that she couldn't survive losing another child. Another death would be the end of her.

Andi glanced at the adjacent empty seat. No Jacob, as usual. Since they moved to Charlottesville last July, he had disappeared into the pediatric intensive care unit at UVA. For all those years of medical school and residency, they'd told themselves their lives would change for the better once Jacob became a doctor. Well, not so much. He did get a paycheck now rather than a meager stipend, which was a nice change, but he still faced long and grueling hours at the hospital, rarely making it to church or Maclain's basketball games or any event that took place in daylight. She stifled her thoughts, which were heading toward irritation and bitterness. Jacob was at the hospital, in the NICU, saving lives. She forced herself to keep that fact front and center.

Andi sat close enough to the stage to see the sweat flowing down each side of Maclain's face. His fine, white-blond hair stood up like a dandelion gone to seed. Maybe static electricity? Or pure terror?

A sudden wave of nausea hit Andi. Maybe it was the heavy fragrance of perfume worn by the woman behind her or the heat of all the bodies crowded together on folding chairs in the gym. She longed for the old days of a real school auditorium, with real seats and decent acoustics.

Maybe it wasn't the perfume or the heat. She'd felt nauseated every morning and evening for the past week. Years ago, she might have assumed she was pregnant, but after years of fertility issues, she didn't bother to entertain that possibility. Probably an ulcer. Last summer Jacob had worked right until the day they left Durham, so she had to orchestrate the whole move by herself. Coming to Charlottesville meant starting all over. She had to settle Maclain at a new school, try to make friends, find a church, locate a good grocery store, and all without Jacob's help. And, of course, Eileen—that dull agonizing ache never left the center of her soul. On any stress scale, she'd earn a fifteen out of ten. She wished she had brought some crackers to settle her stomach.

Time for the big finish. Andi braced herself. Please, God, let it go well. She couldn't bear the thought of a disconsolate Maclain just before Christmas.

Crash and another crash. Maclain and Tim launched into their wham-bang finish. Loud. Completely arrhythmic but mercifully brief. The audience cheered and clapped. Both boys grinned. Andi sighed. Home free.

The next morning Andi woke up feeling intensely nauseated. She sent Maclain off to school and then made a doctor's appointment for the following day.

One of the first questions Dr. Hwang asked was, "Could you be pregnant?"

Andi laughed. How could that be possible?

Yes, she and Jacob hadn't bothered to use birth control since Eileen died. Her doctors at Duke and the fertility specialists at Johns Hopkins clearly had stated that due to scar tissue from multiple miscarriages and an "inhospitable uterus"—how she detested that phrase—Andi's chances of ever conceiving again were nil. Jacob and Andi took them at their word.

Could she be pregnant? Of course not.

After a physical exam and blood test, Dr. Hwang determined that Andi was in her sixth week of pregnancy, due in August. Andi wanted to feel happy. She would have expected that she'd feel overjoyed. Instead, her heart pounded. She grabbed the arms of her chair to steady herself.

Dr. Hwang half stood from behind her desk. "Are you all right?"

"Uh, I will be. I need some time." Andi had no emotional reserves. Grief had depleted and diminished her. She didn't need time so much as a complete assurance that all would go well. That this baby wouldn't die.

That night, after Maclain had gone to bed, Andi poured herself tea and settled into an armchair. As she held the warm cup against her cheek, she came to a decision. She wouldn't tell anyone, not even Jacob. Not for a while anyway. She couldn't bear the thought of walking through another miscarriage with him. She didn't want him to have to worry about whether this baby would survive after birth. Sadly, she knew she could pull off the deception easily enough with his being gone twelve to fifteen hours per day and on call the whole of Christmas week.

She didn't even want to talk with God about the pregnancy. Didn't want to ask that their baby be born healthy and stay alive. She'd spoken those specific prayers for Eileen and she'd received a soul-crushing answer.

The Lord knew what she wanted. He could read her mind. She'd leave it at that. Andi chose not to allow herself to hope.

In her twenties, Andi prayed about everything and made a point of telling everybody that she was praying over everything. At times she felt as if she were managing a heavenly insurance plan for her family and friends. "I'm putting it in the Lord's hands," she'd say, "and everything is going to turn out just fine."

Back then, she took care to differentiate between her deadbeat earthly father, Jack Maclain, and her heavenly father, the giver of good gifts, the answerer of prayers. Her earthly father was in no way like her Heavenly Father. Andi's maternal grandfather, Pop, did not hide his contempt for her Jack Maclain. Pop referred to Jack as that real estate lawyer who "preyed on old people." Pop especially detested Jack because Jack would not allow Andi to call him "Dad" because he felt that being called "Dad" would age him around his many women friends. Pop suggested that Andi call her father "Jack Ass" and leave it at that.

Regardless of her prayers, Eileen died. Over time, with the help of a therapist, Andi realized that she'd forgotten to figure in free will, the fallen state of this world, and the immortal words of the Rolling Stones, "you can't always get what you want."

Andi let her mind wander back to the potential new baby. Dare she even dream that she'd wind up having another child? She'd named Eileen after Leenie, her first cousin and best friend all through childhood. If she were carrying a boy, she'd want to name him after Jacob, but a girl? She pushed the thoughts out of her head. Too painful.

From outside, Andi heard the crunch of tires on the gravel driveway. Eleven o'clock. Another long shift at the hospital. She wondered if Jacob would collapse into bed without thinking to ask about her day.

Andi counted the bouquets. Ten vases of all shapes and sizes sat on the long window ledge in her hospital room. Collectively, they gave off a fragrance reminiscent of a funeral parlor. She wanted to summon up gratitude, but all she felt was exhausted.

Two days before, the baby had burst into the world screaming so loudly that everyone in the birthing room felt fully assured the child possessed flawless lungs. They named the infant Sudie. Andi's choice. No middle name. Not named for a favorite ancestor or an admired famous person. No hopes attached to this name or this baby. It felt too presumptuous to think about the future. Simply Sudie.

This morning, as she filled out an application for a birth certificate, an image of Eileen's death certificate came to mind. In black and white, that single sheet of paper had delineated Eileen's brief life.

Leaning on her elbow, Andi peered over the bedrail to look into the bassinet. Sudie was wrapped snug in a cotton blanket: spiky black hair, ruddy complexion, compact.

Eileen had been blonde, fair-skinned, and long-limbed, looking identical to Maclain when he was an infant. When Dr. Carter placed the squalling infant on Andi's chest, all Andi could think was, "She looks nothing like Eileen . . . ." Later, she realized that Sudie's distinctive appearance was a gift of sorts.

A loud knock startled Andi. Dr. Carter walked in, a chart in her hand. "You get to leave today. Excited to go home?"

As a matter of fact, Andi wished she and baby Sudie could camp at the hospital. At least until the child turned five, Andi wanted to live surrounded by specialists.

"No. Not exactly. Maybe she's too little to leave. She's only seven pounds. Maclain and Eileen were both over nine." Andi took a deep breath, trying to hide her anxiety. Jacob worked with this woman every day. No need to let Sarah Carter know how terrified and out of control she felt.

Dr. Carter leaned over the bassinet and smiled. "Your daughter is full term, petite, and perfectly proportional."

"What about her heart? Did the tests come back yet?" One of the many theories was that a heart defect had caused Eileen's death.

The doctor pulled up a chair next to Andi's hospital bed. "All fine. You've got a healthy baby here. Relax. Enjoy her."

Andi choked up. She couldn't stop tears from rolling down her cheeks.

Dr. Carter took Andi's hand. "Call me any time, about anything. I mean it."

At two, Jacob arrived with Maclain in tow. Andi remembered the moment Mac met Eileen. He had been over the moon. He had burst into the hospital room and started hopping up and down. He had paused only to kiss Eileen's forehead.

This time Jacob had to gently push Maclain toward the bassinet. Her son looked in for a second then said, "That blanket is on too tight. How can she possibly breathe?"

The Next December

Andi's lungs are burning. Can't catch her breath. An enormous dark creature is chasing her. As she runs, she's cradling Sudie in one arm, holding Eileen in the other. She turns, but can't make out his face. She hears growling, hears his footfalls on the pavement. Andi feels his breath on her neck. Suddenly, she's waist deep in water. Her arms grow weak. Her legs won't move. Water rises to her chin now. Two strong hands grip her shoulders, shoving her down. The babies tumble out of her arms . . .

Andi gasped then slowly shook herself awake. She looked to her right. No Jacob. She struggled to orient herself. Then she remembered that Jacob was on call at the hospital. At least he'd have the next two days off, Christmas Eve and Christmas.

And Maclain? That's right, he was at a friend's. Maclain had stayed at Tim's, his first overnight away since Sudie was born. She had to talk him into it. He didn't want to spend a night away.

Sudie!

Andi glanced at the clock: 7:03 a.m. Oh no! Sudie had never slept in this long. She leapt out of bed and dashed to her baby's room. The child lay quietly, staring at a fish mobile floating above her head.

Andi tried to calm her pounding heart. Breathe in four seconds. Hold four seconds. Breathe out four seconds. Repeat.

After changing Sudie, Andi put the baby in a high chair and fed her rice cereal. Sudie opened and closed her tiny fat fists, eager for every spoonful. Andi could hardly keep up. The cereal did not satisfy Sudie, so Andi mashed a banana right onto the plastic tray.

She heard the back door open. "Hey," Maclain yelled, "I'm home." He dropped his duffel bag by the door then rushed toward her and the baby. "Is Sudie okay?"

Andi kissed his forehead. "Fine. How was the sleepover?" She scooped a bit of banana into Sudie's mouth.

Maclain walked up close to the baby's face and peered at her. "No. I mean, how is she, really?"

Andi laughed. "Great. She's an eating machine."

Maclain collapsed into the kitchen chair closest to Sudie. "Whew. I'm glad. I didn't get to check her this morning. I didn't know . . ."

"Didn't know what?" Andi noticed that Maclain's face was all frown and furrowed brow. He stayed silent, rubbing his thumb up and down a groove in the wooden table. "Sweetie. Didn't know what?"

"Eileen . . . that morning with the ambulances," Maclain's eyes filled with tears. He couldn't find words.

Andi stood up behind Maclain and put her arm around his shoulder. "What? You can tell me."

He half stood, pushing Andi's arm away from him. "It's my fault Eileen died. She'd be alive if it wasn't for me!"

"What?" What was Maclain talking about? Andi couldn't wrap her mind around a word of it.

"That day, I was late for school. I didn't go in and say good morning to Eileen." Maclain started to cry. "I didn't wake her and then she died."

"Oh Mac, Eileen was sick. Trying to wake her wouldn't have made a difference." Andi hugged him. "Eileen had a medical problem we didn't know about. Maybe it was her heart. We're just not sure. That's why she died."

Maclain covered his face. "No, it was my fault."

Andi sat in the chair next to him. She lifted his chin to meet her eyes. "It wasn't your fault. It wasn't anybody's fault." Well, God. Maybe it was God's fault. She hadn't figured that out yet.

Maclain stood and walked to Sudie, who had happily plastered smashed banana onto her face and hair. "Will Sudie die?"

No words and a million words rushed into Andi's mind. "Honestly, I don't know. The doctor says she is one hundred percent healthy. But the truth is we all die some day and none of us knows when." Immediately, Andi regretted what she'd said. This boy already seemed to be chock full of anxiety.

But Maclain took a deep breath. He seemed relieved. "Yeah, I guess that's true. Everybody's gonna die some time or other." Maclain sighed. "Still, I kind of can't stop being scared about Sudie."

"Me too." Andi felt a tiny, persistent buzz of fear humming through her body all day every day. She wet a washcloth at the sink then cleaned Sudie's face and hands. "Loving somebody is scary because you can lose them. When you love someone, you risk feeling lots of pain."

"Yeah, that's right. Feeling sad hurts." Maclain took the washcloth from Andi and brought it to the sink.

"I know. I'm sad, too. We can't control what will happen in the future. Though, we do get to choose how we live in the present. I have the gift of being with you and Sudie, right here and now. I'm going to choose to enjoy that gift." Andi liked the sound of her words and wondered if there might be a time, she hoped not too far ahead, when she could fully embrace them. For now, she'd have to take it day by day, maybe minute by minute. She gave Maclain one more hug before he ran off.

After breakfast Andi decided to bathe Sudie. She turned up the thermostat several degrees, creating a near sauna in the kitchen. She placed a large, thick blue towel in the deep, stainless steel sink, making sure to drape it over the counter on either side. She turned on the tap, adjusting the temperature to be warm, but not too hot.

As Andi lifted the child out of her baby seat, Sudie looked into her eyes and reached for her. Andi laid her onto the plush terry cloth, quickly removing her onesie and diaper. Sudie started moving her arms and kicking. Andi smiled to see how happy her daughter felt to be free of clothes.

Andi lowered her wrist into the water. Perfect temperature.

She slid Sudie into the warm bath, making sure to support the baby's neck. Andi used a plastic cup to pour water over the back of Sudie's head and then gently rubbed shampoo into her daughter's dark, curly hair. The baby moved one arm, splashing herself. Sudie giggled and then slapped the water again. Drops of water hit Andi's face and chest.

Sudie discovered both of her arms and she gained momentum. By the third splash, Andi's blouse was drenched.

Andi slowly exhaled and began to laugh.

Mama's Last Christmas, 1953

Elizabeth Doyle Solomon

In big-city New Orleans Christmases of my childhood, no one usually wanted to drive to east Louisiana tree farms. That was true, especially *this* year. We could walk to the nearest tree lot and choose a perfect Christmas tree for our small living room. I was eleven and little brother Paul was ten. It was just one week before Santa's big day, and Daddy had promised. "This weekend," he said, "we'll search for our tree."

This was Mama's third year with colon cancer. At a young thirty-eight, her beautiful ivory face had yellowed and sagged. There were dark circles beneath her eyes. She was so thin that Daddy could easily lift her to the backseat of our 1952 Plymouth. Mama had endured two surgeries by this time, neither of which could remove this cancer, which was zapping her strength and life.

Mama discovered she was pregnant two and a half years before, even as her cancer diagnosis was confirmed. She refused to consider an abortion, even when Dr. O'Neill warned her that pregnancy hormones would accelerate the tumor's growth. She really wanted this baby. In those pre-ultrasound days, none of us cared if it were boy or girl. We all just wanted a healthy baby. And, oh, was Cindy ever that and more! She had a mop of dark ringlets, Mama's dark eyes, and an exuberant personality. She laughed easily and chattered happily in her doorway swing.

Mama sat in the big upholstered living room chair, holding baby Cindy and giving her a bottle. Perry Como sang Christmas hymns on our black and white TV, and Mama hummed along with him.

"Mama," I pleaded, "Will you and Cindy come with us to choose a tree?" I was forever "Pollyanna," catching Daddy's optimism that God would send a miracle and totally heal Mama's cancer. "No, I don't believe so, Betty Ann. I'm content to sit here with your baby sister. She's almost asleep anyway. We'll just enjoy the rest of Perry Como's show."

Daddy took a blanket and covered Mama's lap and legs, and watched as my baby sister snuggled into sleep. He put a warm shawl around Mama's shoulders. "Will you be OK, Betty?" he asked Mama. "I'll be just fine, Paul. You and the kids go ahead to your Christmas tree hunting."

Daddy kissed Mama's pale cheek as we kids threw on winter jackets. New Orleans winters at December's end were usually mild. But tonight's fifty degrees temperature felt very cold and damp, more like the low forties because of this city's famous humidity.

"Brr!" Daddy shivered as he closed the living room door behind us. "Fog's gonna settle early tonight from Ole Man River!" We lived a mile from the Mississippi, close enough to hear ships' foghorns giving their low blasts.

We chose a beautiful Scotch pine from the Desire Street lot, just two blocks away. Daddy also got some pine trimmings to make a front-door wreath. He paid the five-dollar fee and we walked home singing "Jingle Bells."

Daddy opened the door just far enough for Mama to see our tree. Then he propped it on the covered front porch. Paul and I hung up our jackets and started flipping channels, looking for a Roy Rogers or a John Wayne western. Daddy lifted Cindy from Mama's lap and laid her gently in the bedroom crib. Then he gave Mama her 7:00 p.m. pain pill from the little bottle high on the walnut wardrobe. One pill half the size of the hole in my school loose-leaf paper was supposed to last four hours, but it seldom did.

By the time Daddy helped Mama to her bath and nightclothes, it was time for Paul's and my baths. All of us ready for sleep, Daddy patiently lifted Mama into their big double bed. As we did every night, we knelt around the bed and recited the rosary. I always ended those prayers with my own. "Please, God, help Mama to get well. Send a miracle and heal her completely."

We spent the next night setting up the tree in one corner of our living room. We decorated it with bubble lights, ornaments, and, lastly, angel hair. Daddy spread the red and green felt skirt beneath the tree. Then he lifted Cindy in his arms and helped her to put the beautiful white angel onto the tree's topmost branch. Cindy clapped her little hands, and we all clapped too.

The whole family sang Christmas carols and hymns every night, sitting around Mama's blanket-covered chair. Oh, how her brown eyes shone, and how those very thin lips smiled! She put on a good show for all of us, because *I* could see her pain beneath the smiles.

By this stage into her illness, Daddy had hired a housekeeper named Alice. She did all the cooking, cleaning, and laundry. Her lively chatter often brought real laughter from Mama, heard so seldom in those sick-bed days. That good-hearted soul, Alice, stayed with us for thirty years. Her parents had been Holocaust survivors, and she taught me the German alphabet and some German numbers.

One evening, two days before Christmas, Mama asked Paul and me, "Did you make up your lists for Santa? Sometimes he forgets what you tell him at Maison Blanche!" That was the French-named department store on Canal Street ("White House") where Daddy took us to sit on Santa's knee and whisper our secret wishes. Paul and I both got out sheets of loose leaf and wrote our Christmas wish lists. They each filled up a whole page! At the top of my list, surrounded by stars, was my number one wish: a BIG BRIDE'S DOLL WITH REAL HAIR. At the top of Paul's wish list was a ten-speed bicycle.

Cindy was too little to write her list, but Daddy had already made her a "Secret Santa" gift. I wasn't supposed to know, but I had big eyes and didn't miss a thing. In his workshop garage, he had worked for many weeks on a rocking horse for Cindy. It had real horse's hair for mane and tail and was painted red and yellow.

"What's your wish for Christmas, Mama?" I asked her. She closed her eyes and was silent a moment. "Mine's more a prayer than a wish," she said. "I pray that God would heal me completely so that I can continue to be a mother to you, Paul, and Cindy—and so I can keep on loving Daddy." Her eyes filled with tears and so did all of ours.

On Christmas morning, Paul and I awoke early and tiptoed to Mama and Daddy's bedroom. "Wake up! Wake up! Santa has come!" Baby Cindy opened her eyes and grabbed the crib bars as if to say, "Yay! Let's see what Santa has brought to us!" Of course, she had just a minimum of words at two and a half, but her big eyes said it all.

Daddy put Cindy into my arms, and then he helped Mama to her living room chair. Cindy's voice was the first to respond when she saw the rocking horse. "Da-da! Horsie, horsie! Look!" Daddy put her on the rocking horse and she squealed with joy. My own eyes smiled as I saw what Santa brought me: a perfectly dressed bride's doll with *real* hair! And leaning against the couch was Paul's ten-speed bike!

Oh, that joyous 1953 Christmas morning, none of us imagined that it would be Mama's last Christmas. Our prayers and hopes were high, and our optimism was contagious. Even Mama's surgeon, Dr. O'Neill, had his smiles and cautionary projections. "There's never a definite yes with cancer," he had told Daddy, "but your wife has a strong fighting spirit."

That spring Mama had one more surgery. Daddy brought her from the hospital to her sister, Octavia's, spacious home, where Mama could convalesce in a large, cool bedroom with a view of Aunt Tavia's lush rose garden. I was old enough to cut Mama's surgical bandages from rolls into small gauze squares. When she was strong enough, Daddy lifted her again into our Plymouth's backseat, full of pillows, to carry her back home.

Father Dominic, our Parish priest from St. Mary's, came three times that summer to give Mama the Last Rites. Amazingly, she seemed to revive and get better each time. We continued our nightly rosary ritual kneeling around her bed. Daddy simply refused to believe that she would lose this battle, and assured us that God's miracle *would* happen.

But in the first week of August, Mama motioned to me with a weak hand, to come and sit on the edge of her bed. Her words were simple, unexpected, and awful to me. "Betty Ann, Jesus is calling me. I am going to Heaven soon." "Oh, no, Mama!" I cried, tears filling my eyes. "Daddy says you're getting better and that God will send a miracle!" "No, no, Betty Ann. Daddy means well, but *I* know better. Listen! Promise me something."

"Oh, Mama, I'll promise you *anything!*"

"Promise me," she continued, "that you will be the little mother, and take care of Paul and baby Cindy."

"Oh yes, Mama! I promise! But you'll see, you *won't* die!"

I hugged her thin, frail body and we both cried. "We'll have another Christmas together, Mama!" She closed her eyes and

56

pointed to the pill bottle I was now tall enough to reach. I looked at the clock. "Only twenty more minutes, Mama." She groaned, clenched her fists, and bit her lips to keep from crying out.

Mama was right in the end. She *knew* it was her time to die. She breathed her last at Baptist Hospital in New Orleans, only thirty-nine years old, with Daddy, Dr. O'Neill, and Father Dominic by her side. Paul and I were at Grandma Doyle's when the news came. I was absolutely heartbroken. No one and nothing could assuage my grief and disappointment.

But I kept my bedside promise to Mama. Needing a mother myself, I stepped forward and became mother to Paul and Cindy. When Daddy remarried three years later to my stepmother, she was a career Navy nurse with no idea of how to be a mother. When she had her first, and only, baby at age forty-one, I knew exactly what to do when she did not. I became the "little mother" again to my baby brother. In the years since then, Mama has watched from Heaven as I lost two babies, adopted two babies, and cared for thirty-five foster kids.

My promise to Mama led me even farther: to become a pre K-4 teacher, have my own weekly nature camp every summer at my James River farm, and to be a private tutor to hundreds of children with learning disabilities. Mama's last Christmas has carried me on a life-long journey that I could not have foreseen at the young age of eleven. Perhaps it was *her* strength, fortitude, and courage that inspired me. She knew what I had in me, and has watched over three motherless children from Heaven all the way to this day.

New Orleans Christmas, 1947

Elizabeth Doyle Solomon

As I was growing up as a child in my native New Orleans, Christmas always meant going to Grandma Doyle's. After opening Santa's gifts on Christmas morning, we dressed in our Sunday best. Then we walked to St. Mary of the Angels church for 11:00 a.m. mass. After the service, we caught the Galvez Street bus. Mama; Daddy; little brother Paul, aged four; and I could all ride for a total of twenty cents! Daddy let me, a grown-up five, hold the transfer slip, which was good for a second bus and the Carrollton Avenue street car.

In my Christmas plaid jumper, which Grandma's fingers cut from soft corduroy, and my new red blouse, I was a jumble of excitement and questions. "How long will it take us to get there?" and "How many of our cousins are coming?" and "Will the Oklahoma Doyles be there?" Brother Paul's questions were mostly about how the bus doors opened and closed, or the variety of cars and trucks on the streets.

Mama let me pull the streetcar cord for our Carrollton Avenue stop. It was just a short, two-block stroll to Grandma Doyle's house at 8218 Panola Street. When Paul and I saw familiar banana tree plants under the old Chinaberry tree, we ran ahead to Gram's two-story house. We waited breathlessly on the wide concrete steps for Mama and Daddy to catch up. Mama wore a cherry-red, long-sleeved dress, which showed her figure and matched exactly her Avon-colored cherry-red lips. Her wavy black hair framed an ivory face, with flashing brown eyes. Daddy wore his double-breasted gray suit and had just whispered something to Mama that made her lively laughter ring out like bells.

We four crossed the large screened-in porch, and I reached up to ring the black-button doorbell. Beautiful Aunt Mary Lou opened the door, and a chorus of children's squeals rose behind her.

"Merry Christmas, Ho-Ho-Ho!" Daddy's deep bass voice boomed out. A dozen cousins of all ages and sizes met us. "Mom's in the kitchen, Paul," Aunt Mary told Daddy. "We just finished making sandwiches for all the kids." The "local" Doyles and their children had been the first to arrive, like us, on bus and streetcar. For who, in those post-war days of 1947, could afford a car except the very wealthy? Paul and I gave our expected kisses and hugs to the aunts and uncles gathered in chairs and sofas in the living room.

We cousins were ushered into the bright, windowed breakfast room for our lunches, while the adults sat around Gram's massive mahogany table to eat their chicken salad lunches.

I can still smell the wonderful mix of aromas floating in the air of Gram's house: banana oil used to polish her antiques and smells from the kitchen of baking hams, yeast-raised breads and rolls, and a variety of creamy, cheesy vegetables. I was always the one to lift the linen tea towels that covered Gram's pies with their criss-crossed pastry tops.

I listened to the conversations with rapt attention, not knowing then that I'd keep them in my memory-bank for future stories and poems. Gram's voice was front and center from the dining room. "Helen, Burt and children will fly in at 4:00 p.m. from Ohio. They'll take a cab from the airport. Bill and Sue with their boys will come from Tulsa at 5:00 p.m., followed by Jim and Merle from Oklahoma City at 5:30 p.m." Uncle Tommy, as it turned out, would do the airport taxi service for the Oklahoma Doyles, as he was the only local Doyle with a car.

Gram's voice droned on: "Tex, Betty, and little Linda Jean are driving from Houston. They'll be here in time for Christmas supper." Over seventy years later, I can still hear Gram's voice, see the breakfast room cousins, and detect each dining room table adult voice. Florence Farley Doyle had reared an amazing family on the Oklahoma prairie of the early 1900s. While Grandpa used his house and chimney-building skills in nearby Tulsa, Gram birthed eleven children, two of whom are buried beneath the cottonwood tree on their Muskogee farm. On my own Virginia farm, I would be carrying on Gram's traditions of milking (goats, not cows), tending chickens, churning butter, making bread, and caring for adopted and foster children since I could not have my own. I did not know then that I'd be the only grandchild to walk in my grandmother's busy shoes.

After lunch, Aunt Mary Lou announced to the cousins, "Now it's time for the spare-room toys! But first, carry your plates to the kitchen and go down the hall to wash your hands." Every visit to Gram's had surprises from the small, locked room that was called "the spare room." It was full of closets and shelves with doors. Every Doyle grandchild waited with shining eyes for the spare-room goodies.

Aunt Mary Lou (the smallest cousins called her "Woo-Woo"), tall, dark-haired, and beautiful, was the only one of Gram's nine living children who had never married. Though she had several proposals for marriage, and had been given at least two engagement rings, she somehow managed to back out of each arrangement!

All of the Doyle grandkids *adored* Aunt Mary Lou, with her long, red-polished nails and lips to match, her stylish clothes, and her obvious streak of independence. In retrospect, I believe she intentionally put off marriage until it was too late to possibly have children. She relished her position of "old maid aunt," who could treat her nieces and nephews lavishly without having the burden and responsibility of parenthood.

Out came the spare-room goodies! There were Pick-Up-Sticks, a ball and jacks, Lincoln Logs, assorted toy trucks and army tanks, wooden puzzles, jigsaw pieces, and precious old storybooks. But of all these, *my* favorite was the Betty-Boop doll, with her big eyes, mop of black hair, and bendable arms and legs.

"Now," Aunt Mary explained, "You know Betty Ann's (*I* was Betty Ann) favorite is the Betty Boop doll. Since it has her name, she may have it *first*. But I will time her for ten minutes (she took out a real stop-watch) as I do each of you. You know that I mean business, don't you? And you must play fair and not get into squabbles?" We all stood around Aunt Mary, indeed knowing that she meant "business." We all sang in unison, "Yes ma'am, Aunt Mary!" We took turns with our chosen games or toys in one of Gram's many bedrooms off the long hallway that ran back to her sewing room.

Gram had put her prairie skills of making all her children's clothes to good use. Now she had the acclaim of being one of New Orleans' Mardi Gras seamstresses. She created many of the ball dresses for the queens of the parade balls, such as Comus,

Rex, and Bacchus. One of my cousins, Phyllis Doyle Dendinger, and her husband, George, were queen and king of Rex one year. I sat in Gram's antique Morris chair and sewed on the tiny sequins for Phyllis's gown, at the tender age of eight.

Eventually, our allotted toy time came to an end. Dolls, truck, games, and books went back into their spare-room closet spaces. The door was locked, its key returned to some secret spot in Aunt Mary's bedroom. We all waited on Gram's screened porch in the balmy December weather for the rest of the Doyle cousins to arrive. We only saw them at Christmas, especially the Oklahoma, Ohio, and Texas ones. For who could afford flights except once a year at Christmas?

My favorite out-of-state relative was Aunt Helen Doyle Davis from Ohio. She was beautiful, vivacious, humorous, and extremely patient with her brood of three boys: Greg, Bruce, and Dale. This year she would introduce her latest newborn—a girl, Gayle (finally!). It would be my first introduction to a nursing baby, and I could hardly wait to watch. Aunt Helen's boys had all been born in Holland and Germany. She had the "modern woman's" approach to mothering, as I was to identify then, and in years to come.

If Aunt Helen Davis was my favorite Doyle aunt, her husband, Uncle Burt, would rank as my least-favorite uncle. He was in the U.S. Air Force when he married Aunt Helen. I have their wedding picture on the wall in my gallery of photos: Uncle Burt grim in his military uniform and Aunt Helen smiling, stylish, and bubbling happiness. That early 1940s black-and-white photo was taken around Gram's dining room table, decorated with tall white candles, flowers, and a beautiful wedding cake. The thirty or so adults in that photo have all gone to their heavenly rewards.

I wondered if Uncle Burt had changed or not. I had heard the adults say that when they returned from his war duty in 1946, he was more grim than ever. He seldom smiled and had no patience with Aunt Helen *or* their four children. From my earliest memory, he was always called "Uncle Grumpy."

Loud, happy voices entered the screened porch, as memories of them present themselves today. Gram's cheeks were full of fresh joy-tears as she welcomed the Ohio and Oklahoma Doyles and their children, brought to Panola Street by Uncle

Tommy's Nash-Rambler and by a yellow taxi. Aunt Sue; Uncle Bill; and their boys, Bill, Jr. and Tony, climbed out first. They flew from Tulsa, where Uncle Bill had begun a successful sand and gravel business. Uncle Tommy Doyle, Aunt Bev, and their three girls came in next, the local ones who lived in Metairie. Lastly were Uncle Jim Doyle and his wife, Aunt Merle. They had no children, except a much-spoiled, toothless black cat in his twenties. An hour later, Uncle Tex and Aunt Betty Cochran drove up from Houston, with their only child, Linda Jean, adopted as an infant and now five years old.

The Panola Street house absolutely rocked with Christmas joy and happiness. Aunt Helen Brockhouse, married to the tallest Doyle son, Uncle John (six feet, five inches), helped Gram in the kitchen. I wouldn't find out until years later just how good a cook Aunt Helen B. was, while Mama was dying of cancer and she took me in, the summer before I turned twelve.

Last to arrive before the big Christmas supper were Aunt Naomi and Uncle Haskel Doyle. Uncle Hak, as he was known, was born in 1907 in Muskogee and was named for the first governor of Oklahoma, which became a state that year.

Uncle Bill's camera on a time-lapsed stand took the 8x10 black-and-white photo of all the Christmas Doyles. Tallest Doyles stood in back, including cousin Jack, already six feet tall and a law student at Tulane. Children sat or knelt in front. Certain ones stood out, like Aunt Mary Katherine (we called her Aunt Mary K.), with her snow-white hair. It had turned white in her twenties, as so many of the Doyle sons and daughters had. Little did I know then that I would join the silver-haired Doyle ranks at age twenty-five and would stand out in photos just as Aunt Mary K. had.

It was I among all the cousins who helped Aunt Mary Lou to set the long dining room table for the holiday dinner. We put three extra leaves in, which extended it to the dining room's length. Normally that banana-scented mahogany table could seat twelve comfortably. But with the extra leaves, it could accommodate twenty-two adults. From the long buffet drawers, we took a white damask linen tablecloth and napkins to match as well as Grandma's wedding silver from the year 1900. From the glass-fronted china closet, Aunt Mary chose two patterns: one with green-scalloped edges and cream centers; the other plan white with silver trim.

None of the other cousins had any interest in the particulars of setting a Christmas table. Plus, Aunt Mary was a stickler for detail and decorum. I learned from her where to correctly place dinner and dessert fork, knives and spoons, wine and sherry glasses, and napkins. She found tall red tapers, which we put into their crystal candleholders. Lastly, we added a long brass candle snuffer and a pot of poinsettias as a centerpiece.

I heard Gram call my name from the kitchen with its good smells. "Betty Ann," she asked, "you are always the one who wants to watch me make the homemade yeast rolls. If you help me cut the dough for the oven pans, I'll give you dough scraps." How *could* I refuse that request? I watched as she turned the dough in the wooden bread bowl that Grandpa carved from a single half-round of cottonwood. It was twenty inches long, an oblong oval sanded until satiny smooth, and then vegetable-oiled until shiny. On a large wooden board, I used Gram's two-ended cutter to make perfectly round rolls, three dozen of them. Covered with a linen dish towel and set beside the warm stove, they would rise and be baked at the last minute.

While the cousins played board games on the screened porch, I helped Aunt Mary set trivets of all descriptions on the table for the hot dishes soon to be ladled full.

I have a vivid memory of what those Christmas dishes were. Only at special times did Gram make so many, and such a variety. I was always determined to taste a spoonful of each! There was the fat roasted turkey, usually a forty-pounder, a ham with its pineapple-clove trim, china boat full of turkey gravy, crystal glass dish of cranberry sauce, bowl of Gram's stewed apples, mounds of mashed potatoes, sweet potatoes with marshmallows, homemade turkey dressing, and both broccoli and cauliflower baked with cheese sauces. Linen towels were laid in a basket with a "bun warmer," black iron with its own pocket, to keep the three dozen rolls warm.

Finally, I helped with whoever wanted wine, what kind, or sherry. I used a pen and paper with each aunt's or uncle's initials and wrote R for red, W for white, and S for sherry. I added three sets of salt and pepper shakers and two bowls of softened butter.

Children were served first in the large breakfast room, and the oldest always asked to say the blessing. With a lot of chatter and squeals, we demolished Gram's good food and carried our empty plates to the kitchen. While the adults ate, Jack, as the oldest grandchild, was in charge of us in a back room, where he told his hilarious made-up stories.

Grandpa gave the Christmas blessing and then wielded the silver knife and fork to carve the turkey and ham. It was such a lively, laughing group that I heard them from the back bedroom: memories to record all those voices and laughter for the stories and poems I'd write in some future day. At age five, I was already reading voraciously and making up verbal stories for little brother Paul.

When Gram's delicious pies were served, all the cousins were called back to the breakfast room to choose their favorites. There were apple, peach, cherry, pecan, mincemeat, and pumpkin—all served with our choice of either ice cream or whipped cream, or both! This was the only time of the year when Gram made so many different pies!

All of the adults pitched in for the cleanup crew, all except Grandma. She took her well-earned seat in the antique Morris chair, where her tired feet could rest on its pullout platform. Grandpa joined her in a nearby wing-back chair to have his after-dinner pipe.

When kitchen duties were done and leftovers put away, it was time for the Doyles' songfest. With Uncle Tommy at the piano, adults and kids alike joined in singing Christmas carols. It was during that singing that I saw Aunt Mary Lou and her current boyfriend kissing beneath the mistletoe! She married eventually, in her sixties, but that is, indeed, a story for another time.

The Italian Crèche

Olivia Stowe

Emily stopped at her bureau in the sleeping L off her living space while en route to the kitchenette to warm Margaret's tea. She couldn't help herself. She had to open the top drawer just enough to be able to pull out the old worn coin purse and check inside one more time. With the check her nephew, Jonathan, had sent her for Christmas she just might have enough now. And just in time. At least she'd have enough if they had taken their prices down again. This was the last time they'd do so before Christmas, though. It was already the morning of Christmas Eve. Well, if not today, maybe in the after-Christmas sales, she thought—if she was lucky. If someone else didn't buy it before she could.

Yes, it was all there. More than she'd been able to save before. It was such a silly thing to do as much as she had to pinch her pennies, but she'd known ever since it went into the window at Mulberry Junction down in the center of the town in early November that she had to have it. And she'd been holding her breath ever since for fear that someone else decided they also had to have it before she could save enough.

"Are you OK?" Margaret called out from the living area. Margaret had been such a fussbudget ever since Emily had taken that tumble in the early fall. But it was rather nice to have someone fuss over you. Emily hadn't had much of anyone to fuss over her since her parents had been taken together in that flood on the Hughes River—more than fifty years ago now. My, how time flies, Emily thought, with a sigh, as she gently pressed the drawer shut and turned toward her friend.

"Yes, I'm fine, thanks. I was just checking. Now, if it only still—"

"I'm sure it's still there," Margaret said. "I just know it was meant for you. What are the chances it would find its way to a small town like this otherwise? You say you haven't seen one just like the other one in all these years?"

"No, I haven't . . . and I've looked," Emily responded. "It's one of the few nice things we had. It always made my

Christmases so special. But your tea. I came over here to warm your tea."

"Thank you," Margaret said as Emily returned with her steaming cup. "I think it will look just wonderful here. I think we did a great job."

They both stood by the window overlooking the Blue Ridge Mountains, the window being possibly the nicest feature of the chain motor hotel that had been converted into a reasonably priced retirement home in this small foothills town. Emily often wondered why a town this size had ever been envisioned to support a five-story hotel, but she was happy that someone had tried—and had failed. She didn't think there could have been a nicer place for her to retreat to in this time of her life.

The two women stood there and enjoyed their handiwork for several minutes. A small silver aluminum tree from the fifties reached up more than three feet at one end of the oak drop-leaf table Emily's great-grandfather and wife had taken across the Appalachians in a wagon on their grand adventure into the West. Emily's own father had brought it back across the mountains, dismantled and in the trunk of his Hudson generations later and stored it in the attic of their Virginia home on the banks of a lazy stream in a ravine coming down off Old Rag Mountain. It was the only thing from Emily's family that had been recovered after the rogue hurricane had turned the stream into a torrent in the middle of the night and collapsed the house on top of Emily's parents while she was away in her first year at the teacher's college.

Now the tree looked perfect on top of the table set off against the background of the snow-covered Blue Ridge. The rest of the top of the table was now spread with clouds of angel hair. Just waiting for the treasure that Emily had been saving for since she'd seen it in the window of Mulberry Junction a scant five weeks ago. Emily had actually been saving for it for several years, setting aside whatever she didn't need for personal expenses as well as the occasional shortfall monetary gift she didn't turn right around and spend on small notions for her nieces and nephews. Emily just hadn't realized what she'd been saving that money for until she'd walked by the window of Mulberry Junction as they were taking down their Halloween display and putting up their Christmas display.

"I guess I should be going," Margaret said, breaking the spell of their shared reverie. "You'll be wanting to go down into the town. The store will be closing early today."

"Yes, I guess it's time," Emily said, her voice choking from the excitement of making the purchase but edged with the fear that her bubble would burst and either the price hadn't been reduced enough yet or that someone else had snatched her treasure from her. "I'll let you know when I have it. And then I'd be pleased if you came up and spent Christmas Eve here with me. I've also asked Jessica. I know she'll be alone otherwise."

Margaret rolled her eyes, being careful that Emily didn't see her do so. She agreed that Jessica would probably normally be alone this Christmas. The residents here avoided her like the plague. She was loud, grasping, and self-centered—and she had a nasty knack of assessing the cost of anything anyone bought along with the embarrassing talent of usually being right on the money with her loudly announced estimate, which was most unwelcome in a community like this where everyone was living on the sharp edge of barely muddling through. But this was just like Emily. Always giving; never taking. That was why Margaret was so excited about this extravagance Emily was setting out to undertake. Emily needed something expensive and beautiful like this in her life.

* * * *

Emily almost couldn't bear to look at the luminous windows of Mulberry Junction in the distance as she walked down main street from the residence hall into the center of the small town. It was getting dark and another light snow had started. The holiday light display was modest, in keeping with the struggling economy of the town, but the duskiness of the late afternoon in early winter and the snowflakes helped make the atmosphere festive. Anticipation electrified the air. Emily could see it in how alive the town was with activity. And she could see it in the eyes of those passing her by, either en route to last-minute Christmas shopping or on their way home from the stores.

She couldn't help herself. She had to look for it in Mulberry Junction's window when she was still two blocks away.

She couldn't see it, though. For a brief moment she was afraid it was gone, and her heart fluttered dangerously. But then she realized that she couldn't see into the window because a woman and child were standing there.

Ah, yes, it was still there, Emily realized as she drew closer. But her heart continued to flutter and she felt herself trembling with fear and anticipation. Her fear was dispelled as she drew close enough to see that the price had been knocked down to just within her spending capability. This only made her trembles of anticipation increase to take up the slack.

It was gorgeous. The figurines were larger than normal. They were made out of terra cotta and were painted, obviously by loving hand, in several luminous shades of brilliant colors—not completely covered, the terra cotta artfully showing through here and there, but otherwise offset by bright dabs of red, blue, green, purple, white, and silver—real silver that had been applied in molten form to the terra cotta. Emily knew this process had required precision. The silver had to be liquefied enough to accommodate the design, but not so hot as to burst the terra cotta base. Blue dominated for the figure of Mary, and purple for Joseph. The angel glowed with a bright white, and the Baby Jesus shown forth in a rich, deep red. Their faces and hands were designated in perfectly formed applications of silver. Other figures were there too, a whole complement of them—shepherds and kings and sheep and cows and camels and even the donkey that had brought the family to the large, unpainted terra cotta stable that framed the Holy Family.

The Italian crèche was beautiful in its own right, exuding a contrasting feeling of delicacy and strength, earthiness and wonder, but to Emily's eyes it was far more than that. It was as near identical as she could remember across the decades of the crèche that her mother had brought with her to her marriage, possibly her family's most precious possession—beyond each other. Emily's mother had brought it out on Christmas Eve every year when Emily was a young girl and they had put it under the Christmas tree. And it would be whisked away on Epiphany twelve days later. Its appearance and disappearance bracketed the Christmas season for Emily. She had particularly been drawn to the Baby Jesus in his silver and vermillion splendor. And seeing the attraction for her daughter, Emily's mother had permitted her to lift this single figurine out of the crèche and stroke the cool terra cotta and murmur her secret delight to him as he blissfully slept away.

Emily's father had once remarked to his wife that she shouldn't let Emily handle the figurine like that for fear of rubbing the silver leaf away, but Emily had heard her mother respond that Jesus was meant to be shared and that she was just glad that Emily was drawn to him as she was.

The crèche had been swept away in the same flood that had taken the lives of Emily's parents, and memories of it had stayed fresh in Emily's mind, becoming something that she was searching for, some sense to be taken out of a hard life and from seemingly senseless tragedies such as life-taking floods.

Emily had eventually accepted that she wouldn't get the answers she sought out of life; she was just happy that she'd lived long and had been able to touch the lives of so many of her students. And, yes, she was thankful that she had her small apartment in the retirement residence and good friends like Margaret when so many in the world, in this community even, had little or nothing—and no one.

Then the miracle. The crèche had come to her small town and had made itself available to her as a goal she could still attain in her life. And here it was. It was still here and in a few moments it would be hers. Her eyes sought the Baby Jesus. Yes, the same one—at least her memory fought to make it so—its silver and vermillion paint perhaps even more luminous than her mother's figurine. New, probably unhandled by human touch.

Emily involuntarily reached out, wanting to touch the small figure in the manger, even though she knew it was behind glass. Her hand instead touched the matted glove of a child, a hand also reaching out and touching the glass just beyond the grasp of the Baby Jesus. Emily looked down, first at the glove, which was threadbare and had a hole in it here and there, and then at the face of the child. She was no more than six or seven, and her eyes were greedily drinking in the crèche. But not the whole sweep of the crèche; she was focused on the Baby Jesus.

"Come on, Rose, we have to be going," a young woman with a gaunt, haunted look to her and wrapped in a thin coat inadequate to the elements was whispering to the little girl. "We have to get back to give Ronny his medicine. You know we can't have that. We'll come back tomorrow to see it again, if you like. But we've got to go, Rose. The stove will be needing more logs. You know Ronny can't take cold."

"Just a few more minutes, please," the girl said in a sad, plaintive voice. "Look, he looks so peaceful, Mom. He looks like Ronny."

Emily turned away, embarrassed at having intruded in the family scene, even if not on purpose. She entered the store and stood by the front display until the clerk came forward.

As the clerk was taking the figurines out of the window and carefully wrapping them individually in tissue paper, Emily looked beyond the window. The woman was pulling the little girl away from the store, but the little girl was still turned to the window, her eyes glued to the Baby Jesus figurine. Tears streaming down her face.

* * * *

"How could she afford something like that?" Jessica was hissing under her breath to Margaret as Emily was bustling around her kitchenette putting out cups and saucers and opening a tin of cookies. "I saw a set just like it in the window at Mulberry Junction, and it was as dear as six months' worth of fees in this dump."

"Oh, I think it's been in the family for years," Margaret whispered back, doing her best to keep a serene smile plastered on her face.

"Humph," Jessica chortled. "That or on deep discount. It isn't even all there. It's missing the most important piece. There's no baby. Why does she even put it out, when there's no Jesus here."

"Oh, I think Jesus is here," Margaret said in secret delight. "Emily told me she had an opportunity to give the Jesus figure away to someone who needed it. She said something about Jesus not needing to be kept hidden away—needing to be shared."

"How . . . unusual," Jessica snorted, rolling her eyes at Margaret.

"Yes . . . unfortunately," Margaret whispered back, and then turned away so that Jessica couldn't see her mischievous smile.

Time for Grace

Olivia Stowe

I'm not sure when it first hit me that she was no stranger to me, and it took several weeks longer to realize the entire disturbing truth.

But why am I awake and why did I wake to this thought? I don't think I was dreaming anything about this. Or was I? I do remember something like this in a dream, but was that just now or last week? Get a grip, girl. Either snap awake or drift back off into sleep. Angel has buried her furry little muff into my neck. She's tickling me with her whiskers, which is going to make it very hard for me to get back to sleep.

But it wasn't Angel who woke me up. I'm clear on that. It was the sound of a car sliding on the street outside—waiting for the crash that, thankfully, never came. The snow must be accumulating on the street surfaces now. It's going to be a rough night—and even rougher commute for people tomorrow. I don't want to think about having to go out in that tomorrow morning.

I burrow down under the comforter, and Angel goes underneath as well, stretches along my legs, and kneads the flesh of my thigh, demanding attention. I should be blissfully comfortable. But I'm not. It isn't just the cat or the car sliding on the street outside that has me awake. I'm wondering where Grace is and if she's found someplace to keep warm and dry. I can feel Angel's heart racing. Cats must be able to sense the change in the weather—and its effect on people. She must know that the temperature is dropping outside and snow is falling and that this somehow makes the night more dangerous. But maybe that's *my* heart that's racing. I turn to the other side and pull the covers up, but Angel moves with me and, crawling up my body, digs in under my chin.

I'm going to have to stop thinking about Grace if I'm going to get any sleep tonight. But why did hearing a car skid remind me of Grace? Ah, yes, it was seeing that car being towed in the lane beside me as I came home from shopping for Christmas presents this evening. It looked just like Grace's car. The city ordinances were that cars still parked on the streets when snowplows were coming out would be towed if they were in the way. But I don't want to think about Grace. It's the Christmas season. I want to think about that—my favorite holiday season.

Let's see. What has to be done at the office first thing in the morning? The thought is interrupted by the sound of another car skidding, this time the sound ending in a metallic thud—but it just sounds like a hit on the curb at the curve up the street. The sound is echoed by a whimper from Angel. I sure hope that Grace has found shelter. I wonder if she will have gone far from where I left her off this afternoon—beside her car. It was unbelievable what she had crammed into that car. I don't see how anyone can actually live out of a small car like that.

Was the first time I realized it was her when I was strolling down Main Street on my way to having a coffee and reading the paper at the Paper Moon café? I turned the corner onto Main, and there she was, shuffling along behind a grocery cart filled with bits and pieces of this and that. It wasn't so much that she was dirty, but that she looked so like a rag muffin in those mismatched, out-of-season clothes and the straggly hair that hadn't seen a perm in I don't know how long. I wouldn't even have noticed her if she hadn't given me that shy, little smile. She was actually making eye contact. It wouldn't have happened at all if I'd had time to see her coming. I could have avoided it all, if I hadn't been surprised and made eye contact myself.

How do I feel about that? What if I hadn't ever made that eye contact the first time I'd seen her? As it was, my trip to the café was ruined. I'd had to duck into the needle shop after I'd made eye contact with Grace on the pretense that that was where I was headed in the first place. And then I couldn't very well have gone on to the café; she might still have been shuffling around out on the street. I don't know if I'd slipped and given a look of horror when our eyes had locked—or if she'd seen me do it. But the embarrassment of being caught off guard like that . . . . It just made me *so* uncomfortable. We'd been talking about the homeless in Sunday School just the week before, and I'd been so self-assured about my attitudes about these people.

I close my eyes tight and try to clear my mind of all thoughts. This has just got to work.

I must have drifted off to sleep, because time seems to have passed before I am jolted awake. I have no idea what woke me this time. Angel is gone now. Who knows where she must have found more security? I must have failed her somehow as her refuge. Yeah, I'm good at that. Now, I wonder what made me think of that? I turn over again, and then I sit straight up in bed and fluff the pillows.

No, that wasn't the first time. The first time was a few days before at the grocery store. She was sitting on the bench near the front entrance with her shopping cart. That must have been where she got the shopping cart. I wonder whether people steal a lot of their carts and what the store does about that.

I flop back down on the bed in disgust and pull the covers over my head. Who the heck cares? Oh, why can't I get to sleep. There's *so* much I have to do tomorrow. And I'd promised to take Grace back to the free clinic for her results during my lunch—but only because I also was taking Mrs. Wilkins to check her blood again. I'm not sure how I managed to get myself roped into transporting Grace; working with Mrs. Wilkins should be enough. And there's so little time for this at Christmas.

Did I see any sort of shelter around where I left Grace off this afternoon? The snow is going to be drifting by tonight. The TV news tonight said a freeze had been declared until tomorrow morning, that the snow might turn to freezing rain—and they'd warned about the city ordinance to get your cars off the streets so the snowplows could do their work. If Grace was out on the street, did she even know about the ordnance or that it was being put into effect? I wonder if Grace's car will be shelter enough for her. But then, if that car I saw being towed last evening was hers—

As if on cue, there's a strong gust of wind outside that sends the trees rustling, and the first drops that sound much heavier than just snow hit the window. They sound like they're big—and cold. I turn on the light on my nightstand to check the time, and just then the electricity chooses to go out. A great silence, except for the tinkling sound of ice crystals hitting the window. Oh, great, the alarm's going to be off. I reach over for the flashlight on my nightstand, and, of course, it falls into the narrow crevice between nightstand and wall. I fish it out, open the drawer, feel around for my travel alarm, and set it in the wavering light of the flashlight. I'll have to change the batteries in the flashlight in the morning. In fact, I wonder how fresh the batteries in the travel alarm are. I wonder where I've stashed fresh batteries. I wonder if Grace has a flashlight in that grocery cart of hers. O-h-h, I moan, and flop back onto the bed and pull the covers up. Shutting my eyes tight again and trying to purge my mind of all thoughts. It had worked before; it's going to have to work again.

My eyes pop open. Does Grace have anything warm enough and waterproof to wear tonight?

"Oh, it's no use," I yell to the empty apartment. "OK, just bring it on." With that permission, the thoughts of Grace flood into my mind. What was she wearing on her feet when I last saw her? Would I have become involved at all if I hadn't substituted for Brenda at the church soup kitchen Thanksgiving Day and Grace had actually spoken to me as I filled her plate, trying my best not to make eye contact, knowing then that I'd seen her before and unwillingly exchanged smiles? She talked to me; she talked directly to me. Would she have dared do that if I hadn't been surprised into making that first eye contact and being tricked into returning that first shy smile? What am I thinking? Why shouldn't she smile at me when we pass on the street and thank me when I've filled her dinner plate? What's wrong with me? We had been friends; why wouldn't she have the right to speak to me?

The wind comes up and the branches of the oak hit against the window next to my bed. I give up, flounce out of bed, wrap myself tightly in my warm, quilted robe, and pad down the hall to the kitchen for a cup of coffee. I turn on the light in the kitchen and nothing happens. Naturally; the electricity's off, dummy. That means no coffee, either. Not even any coffee, I whine in my mind. I'm beginning to really feel sorry for myself. Well, guess what, there's no hot coffee for Grace, either. So, just stop your selfish whimpering.

Yes, my friend. Well, more an acquaintance, really. But not just another stranger on the street. That was the real shock. And I'll bet Grace knew back there on Main Street when she smiled. She probably even knew it when she saw me avert my eyes and scoot by her at the grocery store. It didn't hit me until I saw her in the free clinic the other day when it was my turn to take old Mrs.

Wilkins in for her blood test. She'd been there, sitting patiently in the waiting room. We exchanged looks a couple of times while Mrs. Wilkins was back getting her blood drawn, and finally Grace worked up the courage to voice a tentative, "Celeste? You *are* Celeste Murray, aren't you?" And then it all flooded back to me. Of course this woman was familiar; we'd worked in the same office for nearly four months. We'd gone to lunch together on more than one occasion. This was Grace what's her name—Grace Jordon.

I must have been in shock, because I didn't respond immediately, upon which Grace seemed to shrink back into her chair. She probably didn't know why she had taken that last swing at the social barrier that had been carefully built between us. I certainly didn't know; at that moment, it was a revelation that I'd ever had contact with anyone on the other side of the bar, let alone a past friendship, even if only a short office acquaintanceship. In that brief, awkward moment, it had all flooded back to me. We'd thought of Grace as the bad news girl. Everything seemed to go wrong around her in the office, and she seemed to be in a daze much of the time. Sometimes she reacted in strange ways, and sometimes she didn't respond at all. I know some of the rest of us thought she was a drinker. And there was a rumor that she was living out of her car. She certainly dressed and smelt like she did. And then one day she just didn't show up at all. When I finally got up the courage to ask, I was told simply that they'd had to let her go. They didn't give a reason, and I didn't ask for a reason. I hadn't even cared enough to ask for a reason. And now, there she was, in the waiting room of the free clinic. And I was here too, trapped until Mrs. Wilkins came back from her blood test.

All of this must have flashed through my mind in less than a second—and I must have said something back to Grace, because the receptionist was coming over.

"Oh, do you know Grace?"

"Umm, yes," I responded quietly through a weak smile. "Yes, yes, we've met."

"Well, do you think you could take her back to Grant Avenue, just down from the library, when you leave then? She's been sitting here for some time and says she doesn't think she can get over there without a ride. We did do some tests, and she probably is still a little weak from that."

What could I say? "Yes, certainly, I could do that. Mrs. Wilkins lives over in that area too." And that had led to further rides, both ways, the last two weeks, as they did test after test, trying to find out what problems Grace had that they actually could help solve. I felt trapped. I had so much to do to prepare for Christmas; I didn't have time for Grace and these trips to the doctor's. And as trip built on trip, I saw flashes of the old Grace I had once known, and I couldn't, for the life of me, think why I had cared so little about why she was fired from our office and what had happened to her afterward.

The snow isn't letting up a bit; if anything, it has become thicker and is building. Normally this is perfect sleeping weather, and just now, just as I am about to return to bed, the lights come back on. I'd forgotten to turn the Christmas tree light off, and there it is, framed in the doorway to the living room, Twinkling its multicolored lights at me.

My mind isn't really on the tree, though. All that I can think of is that cup of coffee; I need that cup of coffee. No, that's not the only thing I am thinking of. I'm thinking that I'm going to be having a nice, hot cup of coffee and Grace isn't. Where's Grace? Did that park where I left her on Grant this afternoon have anything in the way of a shelter? I can't remember. And was that her car I'd seen being towed this evening? If so, she likely didn't have any shelter at all. I kept telling myself that this was her choice—a choice she had made and had every right to make. But I was just kidding myself. I hadn't ever asked her that question— whether she lived that way by choice or by chance. I'd spent no real time on Grace at all, despite those trips back and forth to the doctor's office. I didn't even know what her malady was and whether she was getting better. She certainly had a hacking cough earlier today.

I fill the basket of the two-cup coffeemaker with grounds, and then I hear the meow. I turn around, and there's Angel. I call her to me, and she just gives me a disgusted look and strolls back down the hall to who knows where. I don't know why, but that just makes all of the strength go out of my arm and I drop the coffeemaker basket on the kitchen counter and sink down on a kitchen stool. I'm close to tears. But then Angel returns to the kitchen, walks over and weaves through my legs, and then plops down on her cushion in the corner of the room.

I look up and there are those twinkling lights of the Christmas tree. I am mesmerized by the lights. I pull myself out of my stupor and shove the small coffeemaker to the back of the counter, open the cabinet below, and drag out the twelve-cup coffeemaker and a thermos jug.

A half hour later, I'm pulling up to the curb at Grant Avenue. There she is, over by that big tree, huddled behind a dripping grocery cart, burrowed into the snow, covered by a tarp slick from the freezing rain and with a film of white snow rising half way up its surface from the ground.

"Grace? Grace, I brought you some coffee."

"What? Who? Celeste, is that you?" She emerges from her improvised cocoon and sits there, looking dumbly at my thermos of coffee. I look at the thermos as well. What a dumb idea. She's sitting there, soaked by freezing rain, and all I've brought is coffee.

"Yes, it's me. Come on get up. We're going home. The shopping cart should fit in the back of van."

"What? I don't understand. Home?"

"I don't understand either, Grace, but we'll work it out. We'll work something out. Come on, you're frozen nearly stiff. You'd said earlier today you wished you could see the Christmas tree I'd talked about putting up. Well, I want someone other than me and the cat to enjoy it too. Climb aboard."

From His Father's Arms: Sharim's Story

Carol G. Cutler

(First place, fiction, Blue Ridge Writers Chapter Contest, VWC, 2018)

The rubble and jagged ruins in the street cut Yusef's sandaled feet. As he cradled his tiny son, his voice was strong and determined. "Aleppo will recover; I will never leave," he said to one of the three other men, also carrying babies as they walked. Yusuf could not remember when Syria was at peace. Now Russian and Iranian bombs were brought in to compound the government's cruelty to its own citizens.

"No, neither will I," Yusef's friend said. "I was up late, blasting back at Assad's ground forces with a gun the leader gave me as they approached the eastern city, but I'm glad to be with you today, Yusef, to get the children to safety. Who had the light on last night?"

The force of a bomb demolished a building next to where the families were sheltering. The men knew they couldn't risk being targeted in the basement of that apartment building. With daylight and a reprieve from bombing, the men and children were making their move.

"Everyone knows our neighborhood has to stay dark," Yusef said. "Someone must have been stumbling in from bombing near the market street. We will find out who it was later and warn them. All our lives depend on it."

In Yusef's arms and dressed in a tiny cotton shirt and diaper, the newborn Sharim dozed with the rhythm of his father's walking. His Syrian father was taking him to an underground shelter in the eastern part of the city. The smell of concrete dust and rotting garbage pierced Sharim's nose, and his body, so close to his father's chest, was moist from the heat. The muffled lub-dub of Yusef's heartbeat was the sound of safety and security.

Sharim's mother, Yara, and other women would follow within the hour, if the reprieve held. The parents were never outside together. What if the bombing or a sniper killed them both?

Sharim wiggled and whimpered. Yusef loosened his hold and shifted the baby to his other arm.

"Where's food going to come from? The UN convoy was blown up." Hussein, one of the other fathers, was on the edge of despair. He clung to Yusef's faith and hope today for the narrow ledge that was his sanity.

"I know where some is," Yusef said. "We'll pass by there a few blocks farther on, if I can find the place where it is stored. We'll find the spot on the way to the shelter and come back and dig under the rumble if we have to."

* * * *

Over the next two weeks, Yusef had tried desperately to stay in the city and keep his beloved Yara and Sharim safe. Now their shelters had been bombed and the eastern city destroyed. The men who emerged from the shelters were rounded up by Assad's soldiers. Yusef was separated from his family and taken away in the back of an open truck with ten of the young men in his neighborhood. Yusef's terrified eyes locked with Yara's as they were driven away. Sharim's screams rang in the night. His mother was mute, standing helplessly by the road, numb with shock, in the chaos of the moment.

Refugees poured out of Syria like stones pitching over the jagged rocks of a roaring waterfall into a raging, boulder-filled stream. Fear, horror, mass starvation and pain were part of every day and night. The fate of Sharim and his mother merged with the thousands of other refugees who had fled the Syrian civil war since 2011. Assad continued the torture, murder and brutality in response to the once-peaceful protest of the people of Syria during the Arab Spring. Many of the surviving protestors had become rebels fighting the government, but many who had never been part of the rebel protest were caught in the fighting.

The group of mostly women and children from the city of Aleppo survived for weeks by hiding, by clinging to prayers and caring for each other's wounds as best they could. The freezing temperatures and flimsy shelter made cold and sickness a constant reality. Sharim was nourished by his mother, but she grew weaker and became so ill others had to carry her as they headed north. On their journey, barrel bombs from Russian and Syrian planes continued to drop along roads, so they made their way in rough terrain, staying out of sight.

Near the border with Turkey, in the darkness of night, a group of villagers approached the Syrian travelers in kindness, giving them food, blankets for warmth, and an assurance of medical care for the injured, sick, and dying. They loaded the uncertain, desperate refugees into vans. In the morning, the vans arrived at Kilis, dropping off some of the families where ten thousand refugees were already staying. Yara and Sharim were among those who went to a camp on the border between the Kilis Province and Gaziantep to the north, where there were five thousand more tents. In the hot afternoon, Yara and Sharim stepped onto Turkish soil, bewildered and hungry.

A man, with his head wrapped in bandages and his foot in a cast, was helping construct more shelters. He saw the dusty van arrive and the women and children step off the van. Then he saw his family.

"Yara! Praise Allah!" Yusef shouted from across the road, dropping his work and hobbling as fast as he could to embrace Yara and Sharim. In disbelief, Yara ran into his arms, sobbing with relief and joy, clinging to her husband. Sharim was enclosed in the arms of his parents.

"And the others?" she asked Yusef.

"They are not here. That night we were captured, the truck carrying us out of Aleppo turned over after driving into a hole in the road. I escaped and sneaked back toward the city to look for you. After a few hours, I was stopped again. This time by white-helmeted men traveling to the city from the north. Fearing I would be recaptured, they took me to an area where a group of people were going to be transported to the border."

They felt the tragedy of the uncertain fate of their friends from Aleppo. Yara told Yusef of her group's ordeal as he held his son close again. "Sharim has not grown much and can barely cry now." Yusef's tears streaked his dusty face. He could see many in their group were dying from lack of health care and were near starvation. He took them to the tent where medical aid teams of Doctors Without Borders had set up a clinic.

Yusef found simple shelter for the family and they found human compassion, shelter, food, and health care. Yusef met with the men in planning continued migration from Syria. Yara helped with the teaching of reading, math, and women relief workers from other countries taught the children about the culture and language of Turkey in the makeshift school.

* * * *

Sharim became friends with Sasha, the Russian daughter of Viktor, one of the relief workers assigned to the Middle East area. and the two became like brother and sister. They learned to know refugee children from countries of Iran, Iraq, Jordon, Lebanon, Yemen—all from families looking for safety from persecution and war.

At night, around a campfire, the elders taught the children the names of stars like Arcturus and Sirius and stories of the constellations that had been passed down by their Islamic ancestors thousands of years ago. They taught the children to cherish the customs, language, and religion of Syria, but to open themselves to the people and life that had welcomed them. After the campfire meetings, in the quiet of the night, Sharim thought and wondered, looking at the stars, at the peace he felt when the watched the star bluish white Rigel in the Orion constellation. Sharim and Sasha had long talks. He told her terrible stories of soldiers waging war in his country. "The most important thing I want to learn is how to protect my family and neighbors from harm. My father told me to follow the teaching of our religion."

"When religious teachings are nonviolent, conflicts can be settled by teachings of love and justice. But don't the people who tortured and murdered your friends have the same religion?" Sasha asked

"Yes. A different interpretation. Maybe I can't change the fighting anger and hostility, but I want to learn how to dissolve it when it happens."

"With what solution will that be?" Sasha asked, with a good-natured smile.

"Don't laugh. I'll learn what to do as much as what to say."

"Maybe you will come up with what works, Sharim, but I believe another way to settle conflicts is more reliable—the enforcement of rules set by the authorities of the camp. In Russia, the government controls and protects. Religions are discouraged."

"And you have more confidence in that legal system rather than religion?"

"Yes. Religion serves a purpose for some and I disagree with what took place in my country's history in regard to religion. I'm interested in the study of military science to prevent war, if possible, and to conduct war when necessary."

"When is war ever necessary?" he asked.

"Get real, Sharim."

"I will come up with what works. I will learn the words to mediate aggression between fighters."

As Sharim interacted with the kindness of the people in the camp, he felt the respect of Sasha and his friends. The fear and pain Sharim had experienced in the depths of his being began to be replaced by another consciousness—an awareness of a gift, its meaning buried deep in his consciousness. Sasha watched Sharim's words change anger and hostility that sometimes arose among the children playing.

* * * *

After a year, the family found their way to Antwerp, Belgium. Sharim was now fourteen.

"With Aleppo destroyed, all our family and friends, we'll never return home. Assad remains." Sharim's mother's voice was muffled by sobs in the corner room in the home of Havel and Sarah Levy, the Belgium couple who had taken them in.

Sharim knew as long as Yusef, his father, was near, his mother would be strong. Yara was the family tear fountain, her tears a blessing, really. Never-ending tears flowed from her beautiful eyes like the marble fountain in the center of the town square. Her tears were for all of them, for what they had had to endure.

"It's been six months, Yara." His father's soothing voice faded in and out of the sounds of the crying. "These people are kind. Viktor. Havel. Sarah. We are still finding a way to live in Antwerp." The town was filled with medieval architecture, and in the center of the city, market vendors shouted their produce near the steps of the soaring Gothic Cathedral of Our Lady—a contrast to the refugee camp in Turkey.

Sharim's adjustment to school in Antwerp hadn't been easy. He missed his friend, Sasha, whose father, Viktor, found a way to get the family out of the refugee camp to the Levys in Belgium. The old Jewish couple, Havel and Sarah, were in their late eighties. But Sharim knew Yusef and Yara grieved for the peace that had not come to Syria since they left. They were surrounded by charitable neighbors who were somewhat overwhelmed by the flood of new neighbors who have no shared background, religion, culture, language, or values. Their gratitude to the hospitality of the Levys motivated them to attempt to learn the Flemish language, but their accent that identified them as recent immigrants continued.

Yusef found a job in boat making—they lived only fifty miles from the North Sea— and Yara, besides helping Sarah with cleaning and cooking, taught the refugee community's preschool children. After being home schooled for months, skinny Sharim was beginning to fill out, five feet five inches tall and gradually gaining weight, though he felt himself to be the smallest boy in his ninth-grade class.

The Levys practiced Judaism and their home was one of acceptance and tolerance for other faiths. Sharim's parents had told him of the tragedy of the Jewish people of Europe. The Levys were no exception. They were the last of their family's descendants. The rest hadn't survived Hitler's slaughter.

When Sharim and his parents arrived, Havel had said, "We were homeless, like you are now, but we found help in starting over in the city where we had lived all our lives. There is no mosque here, but you will find an increasing Muslim population. As far as I'm concerned, Allah and Jehovah are the same."

Sharim was not so sure about that, according to what he read in the Qur'an. He noticed that the Levys didn't pray five times a day. They paid little attention to the cycles of the moon that set the time of Ramadan. But they did not serve pork and they fasted once in a while.

Then one day, after prayer with his father as they rose from their prayer rugs, Havel said, "If you are done, Sharim, come with me." In another room in the back of the house, a small altar stood against the wall. "Here's where I pray." As Havel put on his prayer shawl, his deeply wrinkled face was in shadow, but a candle illuminated the words of a prayer in Hebrew in a wooden frame on the wall. 'My life and death in Your hands and all the sorrows of Auschwitz and all wars and guide the moments of my day and night.' "I always end my prayer with this," he said.

"Tell me more about what this means," Sharim said.

"It means a cry from the world was raised up to heaven as millions perished. I learned that the god of life is the same god of annihilation."

"It can't be both, can it?" Sharim said.

"How else can we stand to think about what happened to those who are gone?"

Sharim was silent, trying to think of an answer.

"And so, Sharim," the old man said, "It is between you and me." Then he gave Sharim a tiny turtle carved out of Middle Eastern cedar. "I want you to have this."

Sharim still didn't know exactly what Havel was talking about, and, though he couldn't find those words in the Qur'an, he did try to find ways to become like a grandson to him. He brought Havel's favorite tea in the afternoon after Sarah had prepared it. He went to town with Havel, and he waited as the old man sat around the square and talked with his old friends. Because Havel was unsteady on his feet at times, Sharim saw him safely home. Yusef, Yara, and Sharim decided to become the caring family the Levys would have had if their brothers and sisters had not been murdered in the Nazi concentration camps.

Sharim left soon after his talk with Havel and walked a half-mile toward his high school. He rounded a corner and heard shouting and yelling, a noise he'd grown used to in the refugee camp, but not so usual on the streets of Antwerp. It was always in the background in Turkey. In the desert camp, there was seldom peace except when the stars were out and the elders called the families to sit around a campfire. But here Sharim saw three boys surrounding his thirteen-year-old neighbor, Sofia, pinning her arms to a stonewall. Although she was yelling in protest, no one else was around to come to her defense.

Sharim didn't hesitate. "Hey! Let her go!" Sharim yelled from the street. He knew the boys from biology class—Dimiter, Georgi, and Ivan. He had played football with them.

"Get lost, refugee boy," Georgi yelled back.

As Sharim approached the wall, Georgi and Ivan lunged toward him. Sharim ducked and lunged for their feet, pulling them off balance. They all rolled in the dirt. Ivan came up sputtering. Sharim scrambled to his feet. Dimiter released Sofia, who ran away. Then Dimiter stormed toward Sharim.

Sharim mentally calmed his urge to attack. He'd had to defend himself many times in the refugee camp. He wanted to show the boys the strength that came from the fight to survive. He clenched his fists and the thin muscles in his arms tensed. He scrunched up his face and narrowed his eyes. He stood his ground. Ivan and Georgi stood up.

Abruptly, Sharim shouted "Deescalate!" He held his arms straight out like combat helicopter propellers and twirled his body around twice around.

Dimiter stopped, looked at the other two, shaking his head. He scowled at Sharim. "Are you crazy?"

"Maybe," Sharim shouted, "But I'm using more than my reptilian brain!"

The week before, the boys had been in class when their teacher talked about a theory of brain that included the way different layers of the brain evolved—the primitive reptilian brain, followed by the limbic brain, and finally the cerebral cortex.

The boys took a few steps toward Sharim and kept their eyes on him. "What did he say?" Ivan asked Georgi. "What the heck did he say?"

"Biology!" Sharim shouted.

The boys paused for a moment. Sharim couldn't tell if the smile on Dimiter's face was a smirk or half-smile that meant "We can easily beat up this wimp of a kid, but why bother?"

Sharim didn't have a moment to lose. Another few seconds and their confusion would wear off. He shouted, "Let's go this way!" Sharim turned and headed away from the wall. "To the field. To play football." Sharim took off toward the school where the soccer field was a hundred yards away.

After stomping the ground a few times, they ran after him. "You stupid Arab. You stupid, Arab Jew!" Georgi yelled after him.

Sharim didn't care. It's not the time to correct his ignorance, he thought as he ran. One hand reached in his pocket to make sure the tiny wooden carved turtle was still there. The other hand was pumping by his side. He was running as fast as he could.

He called to them, his breath coming in gasps. "This is between us!" "But you may have to deal with Sophie's parents on your own." He looked around and saw the boys had stopped their bickering. Sharim kept running.

Sharim looked back over his shoulder again to see if they were following.

They were. They all ran to the soccer field and kicked a soccer ball around.

With a knot in his gut, Sharim found his way into the middle of disagreements—what to say and how to use his body in exerting a calming influence. Already his classmates thought him odd, like spinning around and shouting "Deescalate"—a funny word for a kid. He could read the beginning tension with the irritated look, and the subtle smoldering of mood that could make people go quiet. Even his teachers had noticed his exceptional social intelligence, but they were careful not to breed jealousy among his classmates by emphasizing it.

* * * *

"I'm not surprised If he'd be interested in studying peace and conflict resolution. I might can help him get a scholarship for college. I'm actually helping Sasha now finding a spot to study military science now, too. I know a Russian diplomat to the European Union who might help young Sharim."

Yusef couldn't believe the family's good fortune to have Viktor's friendship, whose connections had opened doors for their family.

Viktor called back a few days later and spoke to Sharim. "I found a college scholarship fund for Syrian refugee children at Leiden University College, The Hague. It had courses in international justice, global politics, and earth energy and sustainability. Would you like to apply for it?"

"I would love to. Yes!" Sharim said. "That's only twenty miles north of here."

* * * *

"It was Russian bombs that helped destroy Aleppo and now a Russian doctor gives our family this opportunity," Yusef said the day Sharim's bus arrived in Antwerp to take him to the city on the North Sea, the city at The Hague, known as the "international city of peace and justice." Yusef hugged his son. Yara stood by crying copious tears, but Shari knew his mother's tears were mixed with joy today.

"I carried you as a baby out of the rubble of the bombing in Aleppo, Sharim, and now you are going to college," Yusef said.

Sharim knew the stories his parents told him of his infancy and it was as hard for him to leave the security of home, too.

When Havel and Sarah embraced Sharim in good-bye, Sharim whispered to Havel, "Between you and me, Grandfather."

Shared Oreos

Gary D. Kessler

(First place, fiction, Blue Ridge Writers Contest, VWC, 2019)

The timing had been off all week and it had put me on edge and out of whack. I had a new apartment in the Charlottesville Towers building, thanks to the upgrade in my math teaching job from Piedmont Community College to the University, but the timing was all off. There was a gap of a month between when I had to be out of the 2nd Street basement apartment and when I could get into my new digs. And now that process had gone even more off. Jennifer, who taught in the University's sociology department and who lived in the Walker Square condominiums by the Amtrak station toward the University on West Main had generously agreed to let me stay with her until my new apartment was available. That was all well and good, but now the timing was off with Jennifer too.

She'd dropped me off on 2nd Street so I could finish cleaning my old apartment and collecting last things. She had said she'd pick me up at 4:00—that she had a meeting to attend at the University. But then the owner of the apartment said I'd agreed to be finished with everything and out by 1:00 today. I didn't remember agreeing to that, but it was doable and I didn't want to make waves. I just couldn't wait around on his doorstep for three hours for Jennifer to pick me up. I decided to hoof it to her place.

I think I'd lost track of the scheduling of the apartment turnover because when we set that up I had been reeling from finding out that neither my parents nor my brother, Ted, and his wife were going to be here to help me with the move. My parents were off cruising the Mediterranean and Ted and Sarah had picked this time to see the Grand Canyon. More bad timing I said at the time, although Jennifer had said it was more a case of bad assumptions made before checking everything out. She said it like it was a trait of mine—and maybe it was. I didn't want to argue with the woman putting me up in her small apartment for four weeks, though.

It wasn't that long a walk from 2nd Street to Walker Square on West Main, even though I now had a duffle bag full of "last things" to drag along and I felt grungy as hell in the sweat pants and old plaid shirt I'd been wearing to scrub the decks. I had the key to Jennifer's condo and I was fixated on getting cleaned up and opening a bottle of wine. I'd phone her I got to her apartment to tell her she didn't have to come downtown to pick me up.

I got half way to Jennifer's when the skies opened up in a deluge that had me soaked in ten seconds flat. Bad timing yet again. I was right next to the Greyhound bus station where McIntire Road meets the start of West Main, so I ducked in there to sit the rain out, nearly dragging the old duffel bag on the ground, weighted down as it was by rainwater. The waiting room was crowded and those sitting around in there were pretty scruffy, like I certainly felt after several hours of heavy apartment cleaning in grungy clothes followed by a natural soaking rain shower. Although those traveling Greyhound naturally do dress on the ratty, comfort-emphasized side, there weren't a lot of buses on the schedule board set to leave anytime soon, so I guessed a lot of these folks had come in, like I did, to get out of the rain. And quite a few of those probably were homeless.

I had always shied away from the homeless. It was a mix of feeling threatened and guilty, I think. I almost withdrew from the bus station, but it was still raining hard out there. I didn't know of anywhere else I could duck into between here and Jennifer's place to wait it out.

As I walked around looking for the best of the limited number of unoccupied molded plastic seats wielded together in long rows, I realized I hadn't had any lunch. The door into a vending machine room beckoned on the end of the row I was walking down, so I kept walking into it—still pretty much dragging the heavy duffel bag behind me.

Bad timing again to have decided to go out without my change purse today. I had dollar bills but, as far as I could see, the machines only took coins. I came back to the doorway and called out an "Anybody got change?" query. I could tell immediately that I had phrased that wrong. Everyone within twenty feet of me turned their faces away. They thought I was panhandling. "I mean anybody got coin change in exchange for two dollar bills?" I added, in a somewhat weaker and chastened voice. This at least got a taker—seven quarters for two dollar bills from a well-padded motherly looking black woman who only was able to dig out the seven quarters. So, we both won. She got a good return on her investment and I got a bag of Oreo cookies.

It was only after the money exchange exercise that I saw the money-changing machine in the vending room. Typical of how my day—actually, of how my month—was going. What was done was done, though. The one bag of cookies was all I wanted—just a bit of a sugar fix. I waded back into the mass of humanity sitting in the larger room and who were at least pretending—as I would be—that they were waiting to board a long-distance bus. I found an unoccupied blue molded plastic seat at the end of a row that had an integrated side table between it and the next, yellow molded plastic seat and plopped down. After messing around to get my duffel and the tote bag I was using as a purse protectively nestled up beside my seat, I took a cookie out of the bag as it lay on the table next to me and savored the crunch and sugar surge of it. The Oreos were unexpectedly fresh.

I didn't focus in any way on the man who was sitting in the yellow molded plastic seat on the other side of the side table from me until I saw him, out of the corner of my eye, put fingers in the bag opening, and take a cookie out. My eyes, in disbelief, followed the hand and the Oreo up to the man's mouth, and I looked, for the first time, at his face—and then the rest of what I could see of an older man hunched in a minimally supportive, tired-plastic chair.

He had brazenly taken my cookie and put it in his mouth. You had to be pretty hungry to do that in a public place, I thought. I took a close look at him and gauged him to be one of the homeless people who had come in here out of the rain. I had thought I'd be able to pick out the homeless by their scent. It embarrassed me to think that, but there it is. I did. I didn't smell anything off-putting, though. I realized that had been my major concern in picking out an empty chair. I also realized that after five hours of scrubbing floors in my sweats in my old apartment didn't make me smell like a Paris perfumery myself.

He was old and bearded, his salt-and-pepper hair unruly and tossed by the rain, much as mine must be. He, not surprisingly, was gaunt—thin and wiry, and was dressed in just a soggy, misshapen T-shirt, shorts, and tennis shoes that looked like they'd been dragged through the mud. Like the other homeless probables in the waiting room, who were staring out the front windows and waiting on the rain, he had a stuffed gym bag in front of him, pulled into the front of the seat and protected from the world by his thin, sinewy muscled and blue-veined legs. I couldn't gauge how old he was. I assumed the homeless aged quickly. He held a hand towel and was dabbing ineffectually at his wet clothing.

He gave me a shy look—a tentative smile—like he knew I'd caught him filching my cookie and that had embarrassed him. Good, he wasn't so far gone into the off-the-grid world that theft didn't embarrass him. I quite demonstrably pulled an Oreo out of the bag and munched noisily on it, making a humming sound, while looking, not directly at him, but just by him, past his right ear, as if checking the rain beyond the front windows. It wasn't a direct challenge of him—not really. I assumed that would take care of that.

It didn't. A few minutes later, when I went for another cookie, my hand encountered his already in the bag. We both drew back as if we'd received an electric shock. I wanted to give the man a dirty look, but I didn't want to engage with him. I wanted him to leave my cookies alone—not to violate what was mine—but I didn't want it to go to confrontation. With a huff, I turned the opening of the bag toward me. My instinct was to take the bag into my lap, but I wanted him to smooth over the violation and acknowledge the rights of ownership by leaving the bag right where it was.

And then I felt miserable. The man was homeless. He was thin as a rail—and old. I had so much and he must have so little. I was being a real bitch for no other reason than I was feeling off balance with timing problems in life. All of the changes in my life were good; they couldn't be in his life.

It was just a few cookies. The bag had claimed it was two servings.

I couldn't engage with him, of course, but I could make an attempt to be human. I turned the opening of the bag more toward him, gave a little smile, and gestured for him to help himself. He showed me the shy smile again, looking at me and the bag tentatively, and then looking away. But I gestured again when his head swiveled back, and he took a cookie.

The next time we both were reaching for the bag and our fingers touched, although we both recoiled a bit again, it was more comfortable and with a shared chuckle. We each took a cookie, and I now was feeling a lot better—better than I'd felt about myself all day. All week even.

A somewhat fuzzy announcement came over the intercom system. That there would be a public announcement at all was so surprising that a buzz rose in the waiting room, where most weren't really waiting for a bus, and I caught only snatches of what was being announced. I understood more of it than the man next to me did, though.

For the first time he spoke. His voice was surprising: low, rich, cultured. I had an immediate flood of thoughts of wondering how someone with an educated voice like that had become homeless along with a flash of the thought "there but for the grace of God . . ."

"I didn't catch that. Did you?" he asked.

"I think they were announcing a bus for Washington, D.C."

"Ah," he said. "That wouldn't be me. I'm taking the bus across the mountain—to Waynesboro, Staunton, and Harrisonburg. And you?"

"I'm just getting out of the rain," I said.

"I'm without transportation and need to get to Staunton," he said, as if I needed to hear a reason he was taking the bus.

I didn't follow up. I didn't really want to get into a conversation with this man, but at the same time I felt relief that they hadn't called his bus. I didn't want him to go until I'd fully made up for having become cross with him. It was just a small bag of cookies. I turned the opening of the bag to him and, though I found it difficult to talk, said, "Here, you take the last one."

"I've had enough," he answered. "Please, you take it." It remained in the bag.

We sat in silence for a few minutes. I wanted to speak. I wanted to ask him about himself and how he had come to this state of homelessness. I wanted to ask him what there was in Staunton for him. Was it just another homeless shelter and soup kitchen? Did he have friends or family there? Did he need money to get someplace safe? Another fuzzy announcement sounded, and we looked at each other, him questioningly? He was trusting me to have an answer.

"Just an announcement about a lost purse," I said. "They were admonishing us to keep a close track on our things."

"Ah, yes, possessions," he said, taking a look at my duffle bag, which I was pulling in closer to myself in response to the announcement, although I don't know why. All of the stuff in there were things I almost hadn't bothered recovering from the old apartment.

As if he could read my mind, he then said, "Are you waiting for a bus too? Or do you have a place here?"

"I'm between places," I said, "I'm moving up in situation."

"That's good to hear. I'm glad you can have a positive outlook on life," he said. "If it's not working in one place, it's good to just move on."

"I'm living here," I amplified. "I'm not waiting for a bus. Just coming in from the rain. Actually, I—" But before I could give more of an explanation, the loudspeaker had started dispensing its fuzz again.

He looked quizzically at me, his now official interpreter.

"Richmond. The bus for Richmond is boarding," I said.

"Ah, Richmond," he said. "Last time I was in Richmond, Avis was with me. We went to Marymount. She loved the gardens there."

"Avis?" I asked.

"My wife. She's gone now. Last spring. Not many left now. Lionel, my old tennis partner is about the only friend I have left now. I come over the mountain every chance I can get to catch up with him. You? You have family or friends you can go to? Oh, look. It appears to have stopped raining."

"No. None here." My first thought had been that my parents and brother were off on vacation and not here to help me with this difficult move. It was only sometime later that it occurred to me that the man would have connected my remark with a wife and friends who had died.

I wasn't in a hurry to leave. I did, in fact, have the urge to continue the conversation now, to open up more to him and to find out more about him and his situation. But just then, as others who had just come in to get out of the rain were rising and shuffling toward the exit, a young man in a suit was coming into the bus station waiting room, swimming against the exit stream, and looking around. He called out a name, and the man sitting next to me turned his head and half rose from his seat.

"Mr. Winthrop," the newly arrived young man called out, and then when he saw my plastic-chairs companion, he said, "Ah, there you are. I'm glad I caught you before your bus arrived."

"Here, I'm over here," my companion said. "Did you find what was wrong?"

"Yes, and it was nothing, Mr. Winthrop. The mechanics said it was just a warning light going haywire on your Mercedes. Just a quick fix. Nothing was about to explode. It's out front. You don't need to take a bus home. If you'll drop me off at the dealership, you can be on your way."

"Terrific," the newly named Mr. Winthrop said. He leaned over and zipped open his gym bag to put away the towel he'd been dabbing himself with. I could see two tennis rackets and a couple of cans of tennis balls in the bag—no "the only possessions he had left in the world."

I wanted to both laugh and cry, but it came out in a snort. More than anything else I wanted to say something to him, to apologize or something for forming the wrong conclusion about him. But the car dealer man was talking to him, drawing both his attention and his body away from where we'd been sitting, sharing my bag of Oreos.

And then I was alone. There still was a cookie in the bag, but I wasn't hungry and the Oreos had lost any importance anyway. I didn't know, really, what I was, other than chastened and quizzical. I scanned the now nearly deserted waiting room, now longing some connection that wasn't there.

But then he—Mr. Winthrop—the elderly tennis player with a Mercedes—was back, standing in front of me and saying,

"Thank you for sharing the cookies with me. I was feeling a bit lonely and lost. I'm a little hard of hearing and couldn't make heads or tails of those boarding announcements. I hope that it's all uphill for you from now on. Hang in there on life. And, here, another bag—all your own."

Then he was gone, and I was looking down on the side table at a fresh bag of Oreos. It was open at the top, though, and when I picked it up, a folded wad of twenty-dollar-bills slipped out. Sixty dollars.

He had thought *I'd* been the one who was homeless.

The revelations didn't stop there. When I went to put the bag of cookies he'd just given me in my tote bag, I found the unopened bag of Oreos I'd bought. Those weren't my cookies on the side table between our chairs that I'd first wanted to fight over before deciding to be human. Those were Mr. Winthrop's Oreos that he much more graciously had shared with me.

I didn't know whether to laugh or cry—so, as I left the bus station and resumed walking to Jennifer's apartment, I did a bit of both.

POETRY

Recipe for Louisiana Thanksgiving

Erin Newton Wells

(First place, poetry, *Skyline* Winter Holidays Contest, 2019)

It starts this way. Make a roux. Brown butter
in a black iron pan until angels touch down
on your shoulders. Add flour. Brown this, too,

but do not burn. You will know when done
by the way they break into syncopated tunes,
snap their fingers, and tap those delicate feet.

Then the holy trinity—onion, pepper, celery.
Can you smell it now? Angels cry for joy.
Listen. Your ancestors applaud, sing praises.

Pepper and salt, as needed. A dash of tomato,
your mother prompts, so it does not look gray,
though some would call this outright heresy.

Now for the oyster liquor. It turns the roux
into a ballad of love. Now oysters, just until
they ruffle at the edge like Mardi Gras floats.

Fold in white rice. None of that bread dressing
in this house, not for a day of giving thanks.
Oyster rice. Serve it in your best dish. That one.

Grandmothers dance a two-step with angels,
a fine fais do-do to squeezebox and fiddle.
Now bow your heads. Pass the plates. Begin.

A Litany for All Souls' Day

Erin Newton Wells

November, a wet wood. Leaves turn to leather,
the ground a troubled fever of faint cinnamon
on the cool blade of air. A creek to cross,

its shallow water clear as tea from mineral,
too cold for bared feet this day. A field, a stand
of spruce to shield you, a gentle rise of earth,

a plot newly closed, the grass dry, not yet
enough to cover you. A simple stone,
your name incised in keen, quick strokes,

the center of this fold of hills and lowered sky.
I say your name this day of names, again
I say the syllables alive each time I name them.

A Few December Traditions

Erin Newton Wells

We start the new thousand-piece puzzle
with our own versions of carols

well into the night, homemade lyrics
beside the clumps of clay a son once called

snowmen, the yellowed snowflake
a daughter cut too large, and the ornament,

broken but still hung because the one
who gave it is gone. Later we smooth paper

and ribbon and fold it with the tags
left on so they can speak their love notes

to each other a little longer until we need it
again. And even then we tear them off

and cannot bring ourselves to throw away
the names in their gentle script.

Janus Face at Year's End

Erin Newton Wells

We go out for awhile, come back to the house
and raise glass flutes by the stem.

Bubbles rise and pop into nothing.
A new pair of zeroes refreshes the clock.

I open windows to muffled fireworks downtown
and peals rung from a tower

where a lady strikes batons and moves heavy bells
hung above, her body bent double.

It cannot be many more years she climbs the stairs.
Someone else will learn to do it.

Someone else will go out and come back
to the house, touch glass to glass so they ring.

You say bubbles cause the musical sound.
Someone else will say this, too.

Remember how fresh linen smells,
a cloth snapped smooth, an invitation to a feast,

a room, a door looking in and out,
the guest who might come.

Wheatfield with Crows

Erin Newton Wells

(First place, Elizabeth Neuwirth Memorial Contest, Poetry Society
of Virginia, 2019)

Vincent van Gogh, oil on canvas, 1890

> This double square laid on its side, this cloth,
>   this linen stretched to cover it becomes
> a window view, this high wide strip of sky,
>   the deathly midnight dark of blue with black
>
> stirred in that mercy left and rose and turned
>   to night, the hot demonic day below,
> the clots of angels struggling up to pound
>   the portal overhead, their shoulders thrust
>
> against it, pounding fists at heaven sealed
>   and shut—Let in, Let in—this turbulence
> of heavy angels, wings and garments snarled
>   in cloud, the clouds a weight of tumors hung
>
> above the field and boiled and formed of it,
>   the field a burdened endless ache of wheat
> in yellow chrome so reddened that it seethes
>   and makes an illness of the earth, the grain
>
> a gouge of spilled and writhing waves, a churn
>   of yellow heat in buckling heaving plains.
> The field erupts in stalks and seed, a dry
>   and rustling sea to scythe, to lay the grain
>
> in rows of bitter dust. And underneath,
>   the earth in weary nightmare dreams again,
> again, again this scene, an endless vertigo
>   of tilting roads that lead it round and back

and in and up, the gash, the path of dirt,
        a tang of burning acid green, chrome green
of grass that seers its jagged hook, the scar
        it leaves and ends itself and perishes

in wheat, the weight of angels just above
        and pressing down to push, to lift themselves
from earth. And all of this has made it split.
        The crows, the lot of them now come from it.

The crows come out in swarms above, below.
        A hand flings out dark seed of them, dark grain
to sow, dark chaff to thresh, to slash the sky
        as they fly toward and rush the window frame

or fly away. They catch in webs of storm
        to drag it down. A flight, the storm dark black
of crows is born of this, the troubled sky
        in thunder slung above vast fields of wheat.

Their wings are knives, their feathers keen to slice
        the air, cut though, bring rain to boiling fields,
the coils of wheat the earth hauled up to seek
        relief. Cut through the hard and layered blue,

the wheat in dust, in thirst, the earth in need
        of cool remembered mercy as it smooths
the dream from foreheads, as it rests and cools
        the fevered lids of eyes to bring them sleep.

A Chinese Birdcage

Erin Newton Wells

(First Place, Joe Pendleton Campbell Prize, Poetry Society of
Virginia, 2019)

Bonaparte on St. Helena, South Atlantic

> At the approach, a black volcanic rock,
> small, thrusts from the sea, only the sea
> around it. The black grows lion brown
> in parts when near. A green valley swings
> into view. The harbor comes to life at sight
> of the ship. *This cursed rock,* a last place
> to stash him so he cannot get away one
> more time and recoup, an outpost farthest
> from the center of things. Perfect prison,
> nothing but ocean. The Portuguese once
> found it quite by accident, no human on it,
> a minor lump of basalt, hard wart of lava
> spewed, cooled, named on the feast day
> of the saintly mother of a Roman emperor.
>
> Keep him here so he cannot carve empires
> from the world and play Caesar, Hannibal,
> Alexander. That portrait at the alpine pass,
> cape swirled, horse reared back—all show.
> Someone else sat for it, the face imposed,
> while he busied himself, while he lifted
> a king's head where it fell into the basket
> under the blade and put it on his shoulders.
> Here he may stand on a dark edge of rock
> in his tight little suit, a bicorne hat, island
> mist around him, no substitute available
> as the artist portrays him. He surveys his
> ocean kingdom as far as he can see, runs it
> through his fingers now and in his sleep.

Caligula. He does not sink to that, a chariot
into the sea to battle the waves, full bushels
of shells gathered as spoils of war. He learns
it ends here, not even his family allowed,
beloved empress and the son declared King
of Rome. Her likeness hangs on the wall,
a bust of the child on the mantle. A few
courtiers and retainers keep him company,
jailers, house fit with these last treasures,
though rats trouble it, the mold and damp.
A birdcage is ordered for his entertainment,
something to cheer him, to watch, elaborate
plans drawn up, built by Chinese workmen
when they finish the house. Trapped fowl.

A mini Versailles, a Fontainebleau for birds,
the many narrow wooden rods, partition
on partition to move as corridors and rooms,
perch and roost. Gaudy and large. The size
affords no space for flight, only incessant
waddling back and forth with wings folded,
the peck and scrape of beak and claw. Glum
silence sets in. Bird gloom. They can tell.
Not much variety in the dusty troops here.
A maimed pheasant. Doves. A chicken hen.
Exterior painted red and green, those large
animal feet to hold it up. They grip a floor
that tilts on the sea. Roof with pagoda trim,
dragon flames, clouds of forbidden cities.

Embellishments from the countries he might
have owned, given time. Were the workmen
paid. Do their families wait. A death mask
shows a smooth brow, a face corrected into
peace. An amateur's portrait has it in profile,
shrunken, gray-white with cancer. No laurel
crown, no ermine. He said to free the birds,
that the island had no need of more prisoners.

Drink and Be Whole Again

Erin Newton Wells

(First place, Elizabeth J. Urquhart Prize, Poetry Society of
Virginia, 2019)

Frost's home, Franconia, New Hampshire

> This year I watch the world fall in pieces.
> You grow thin, your face cool
> as we lose you. Words seem confused
> on your lips. I lean to hear what you ask
> in whispers, that I must carry you
> to a quiet place. *You know*, you say.
>
> *His place. Be whole*, then leave it for me
> to remember where he went to become
> himself, to guess the road we took.
> How easily lost, a cloud of grief on me,
> space beside me where you ought to be.
> I take all the wrong turns.
>
> Near evening when I arrive, the land
> opens out against a shadow of mountains,
> fields softened to blue where he walked,
> took soil in his hands to feel for moisture,
> where he sat and looked and breathed.
> No one else here now.
>
> I offer your absence to this quiet hollow
> you might want to inhabit. Will it do.
> Is it enough to smooth out
> what came so hard at the last. Will he
> pass by, vanish, reappear and take you in
> where the world stays whole.

The place floats slightly above ground,
a white barn with a scent of bruised fruit,
garden of spectral blooms, pastures,
ruined orchards. Edges dissolve, a blue
unearthly air to scoop, drink, hold you
to me no less because the body fades.

The Wasting Hydrangea

Erin Newton Wells

(First place, Karma Deane Ogden Prize, Poetry Society of
Virginia, 2019)

My grandmother would say they languished,
as women did who lay in the afternoons
with cool cloths on their heads and took
tincture of laudanum. The blue drains
to the edge and to the fine flora of veins,
too much shade, too few minerals, poor soil
at the back of the house. When I am stronger,

ripped open to bring you to light, stitched
together again, I will carry you there,
your weight as nothing and the veins blue
in your fragile skin. You slide into the world,
my blood still on you, cell of my cell,
air of my lung. I will show you these faded
clusters with their old lady look. Some swear

baths of copper salt poured on the ground
enliven the blue, or blue dye from eggs
with its strong vinegar. Or that it may poison.
Or the whole root may be dug and moved
to new soil, a place of better light, the air
cleared of shadow, the ground without
a silent mold that lingers. Fledglings come

to window glass by trees where hydrangeas
languish and dash themselves on the hard
transparent sky. I find them fallen, stunned.
Soon you will grab at everything with your
delicate fingers, put it in the mouth, spit out
if bitter, or swallow. You will soon try it all.

Nevertheless, Isabella Gibbons Reads

Erin Newton Wells

(Jefferson Madison Regional Library/WriterHouse Prize, 2018)

. . . if any white person . . . teach any slave to read or write . . .
such person shall be fined . . . .
—General Assembly, Virginia, April 7, 1831

What you will not see behind curved walls
in pieced garden patches unless
you give a careful look, or even then, behind rows
of columns and houses, the great lawn stretched

in morning sun, what possibly you cannot see
are pinches of seed in her apron pocket.
When she beds them in dark dirt,
warm enough in April and smelling of rain,

roots grab hold, plain hulls show what they hide.
Stems, new shined leaves, come summer,
alive in hard bits of nothing
in this small plot allowed. They want to spread—

mustard, mint, gourd, a bush of peppers curled
with dangerous heat. The bean
pulls itself up on poles leaned together.
In her pocket, a paper folded to fit the palm,

rows of names. Gourd, mint, mustard, and bean.
Or Isabella, one letter borrowed
from mint, two from mustard, three from bean.
Secret, except William knows,

though another owns him,
a time for the ground to make something of it.

(Gibbons lived as a slave at the University of Virginia, owned by a professor's family, but secretly taught herself to read and write. After freedom, she established what would become the Jefferson School for other freed persons. The gardens in back of the pavilions were often used then for slave quarters and their vegetable patches.)

As It Curves Beyond Memphis

Erin Newton Wells

(Second place, Brodie Herndon Prize, Poetry Society of Virginia, 2019)

. . . the arc of the moral universe is long, but it bends
toward justice.—MLK, JR

They used to say if birds fly over your shoulder
on the right side, it means a good day ahead.

If sun falls at the door, the right road waits outside.
So go on and take it. Go on.

A bird sings notes going up, not down,
you know it for a sign.

Go around ladders, not under. Avoid thunderstorms.
Keep out of leaky boats.

If a child smiles at you, it means hope like a child.
Even so, sometimes a child is plain tired.

A town like this makes music curve over the earth.
It could change things.

Sometimes you go out, thunder overhead.
Ladder on the walk. Boat full of holes.

Bridge to cross. Air dead quiet. Sometimes you put
your body in the way because children

want another story and want you to tell it.
They bend you to them like music

if it keeps on far enough, if it does not choose
to stop when it hits a wall,

an injured bird they can hold to themselves
and still hear its voice.

(April 4, 1968, Martin Luther King, Jr., shot and killed in Memphis.)

My Grandparents' House

Erin Newton Wells

(Second place, Loretta Dunn Hall Prize, Poetry Society of
Virginia, 2019)

The place still stands, the dirt oiled where he parked
in the back yard, a deafening of cicadas,
no one home anymore.

But in these shadows he lets me make a nest of sweet
wood shavings by his work bench in the shed
and calls me *Birdie* when I settle in.

On the gray span of porch a passing breeze of him
opens the door, sleeves rolled on his white
Sunday shirt in the heat.

I enter the cool watery depths of the house, the table
set with moonstruck plates, worn silver.
He seats me on thick books.

Before me, a dish my size, the small round spoon,
a face of tarnished dents on it, the food
stewed to surrender.

Brass chimes warble the quarter hour. And she,
who never sits, scurries to feed us,
a wild look in her eyes,

a remnant of horses far away from here, a dream
of lush fields she gave up for this, an oil town.
Fly up, Birdie, he says,

patting beside him on the chair, and I slide into his
tolerant arms. In the kitchen, she scours down
beneath the sink's worn glaze.

Sliding from the Edge of the World

Erin Newton Wells

(Second place, The Writer's Eye, Fralin Museum of Art,
University of Virginia, 2019)

(Based on *Man Reading, Monhegan*, by Jamie Wyeth, 1974, the year
when Watergate weighed heavily on many.)

Take a look. This seems a house sunk in rock.
A third of what you see is adamant,
bald and slick and spattered, a house locked

between rock and sky, this odd clumsy tent
of a roof with a slab of chimney split
through it to hold it, the bleached roof rent

so sky falls in if it chooses, and does not, lit
with high indifference of cloud clumps
in their moody Maine weather, a world slit

sideways with rock, sea, sky. The sky slumps
into the sea, no, stops short of it, a slight
strip of afterthought, nothing much to jump

into by the looks. Its grayed blue runs right
through those skewed windows, as if it might

keep the house from lurching left. The sight
of it all, precipitous, this atmosphere
of tension. Look to the right, someone at tight

quarters, a man with his whole face sheered
to have him anonymous, both armless
and legless, with barely a chair given, a mere

lump. But reading, we are told—no guess
otherwise, no book in sight. Does it lift
his spirit in this corner of doom, a small yes

to the great no of sinking deeper into a rift
of cold rock, the book as a useful wedge
to keep him visible, a raft to help stay adrift

in drowned rooms, year of scandal, hedge

Christmas Letter to My Sister

Carol G. Cutler

(Second place, poetry, *Skyline* Winter Holidays Contest, 2019)

Fresh cut pine tree,
Ornaments from 1940s,
Loving memories for me,
Tattered junk to you
You never wanted them.

And yet you sent to
My daughter a trinket
From China, "For your
Christmas tree," you said.
We miss you, dear auntie.

We live on different continents
And the customs of your culture
Separate you from her and me;
Yet, you still give a thought to
Our family traditions of Christmas.

I think of all we could
Have been to each other,
Still be to each other If not for
The waste of kinship's hours.
You are there and I am here,
My Christmas greeting to you.

Solstice Song

BAMorris

(Third place, poetry, *Skyline* Winter Holidays Contest. 2019)

Sing a song of Winter,
  a whisper on the wind.
Promises of changes
  now wafting through the air.

Sing a song of resting
  of every living thing.
Season of the nighttime,
  of dark and dreary dreams.

Sing a song of dying,
  of leaves and flowers gone:
Of bare, stark, sleeping trees
  and bitter, bruising cold.

Sing a song of welcome,
  breath smoking in the air.
Dance the Winter Solstice
  all voices lifted loud.

Sing a song of humans,
  wrapped like Christmas gifts.
Presents for the Ice Queen
  when she comes sweeping in.

Sing a song of Goddess
  with flowing, frozen hair.
Ruler of the North World,
  all cold and ice and snow.

Sing of celebration!
     preparing for the change.
Only after Winter
     can Spring be born again.

A Christmas Morning Memory

Elizabeth Doyle Solomon

(Honorable mention, poetry, *Skyline* Winter Holidays Contest, 2019)

We were hiding in the music room
when our four-years Shawn tiptoed downstairs;
her fuzzy slippers made not a sound,
excited eyes of us unaware.

And then the squeal, "Oh, Santa has come!"
our camera catching her delight—
when she saw empty plate and milk glass,
"He ate the snacks we left him last night!"

Then we three sat crosslegs 'neath the tree,
(two watching Shawn's face discover the toys)—
baby doll with real hair, carriage too;
"Did *you* hear Santa? He made no noise!"

Wrappings and bows now littered the floor,
and our child's rosy cheeks showed pleasure—
it's been forty-eight years since that day,
dug up each Christmas, buried treasure.

My First White Christmas

Elizabeth Doyle Solomon

I came to West Virginia a young bride
from New Orleans, where I never saw snow.
My first white Christmas it snowed twelve inches
and the mercury dipped to six below!

Raincoat and galoshes just wouldn't do,
so I bought fur-lined boots with jingly bells—
examined each fine flake as it melted,
faster than any Christmas carol tells.

Homesick, I listened to familiar hymns
and whipped up my very first fruit-nut cake—
husband tracked in snow with a Scotch-pine tree;
we hung each ornament with small heartaches.

New love and kisses that snowy winter
helped to take our homesick tears away—
although it was fifty-three years ago,
I remember that Christmas 'til this day!

A Christmas Reckoning

Elizabeth Doyle Solomon

The days, weeks, and months unfold,
'til another year is told—
while we, blind with busyness,
time's passing can merely guess.

What have *I* done for others,
my unknown Christian brothers?
Have I fed a jobless man,
clothed a child in freezing land?

Even *here*, beneath bridges,
our homeless sleep and shiver—
do we say, let *others* give,
that these poor souls may live?

Christ came at Christmas to teach;
we all have long arms that reach
and tongues to tell of His birth,
peace and good will for this earth.

The Christmas Story

Elizabeth Doyle Solomon

Once every year we hear the story,
how three Wise Men followed that Star—
on camels' backs over dry deserts
to find Infant King—how poor You were!

They brought their gifts: gold, frankincense,
knelt before Him with Joy in their eyes—
did they know how He'd die at the end,
crucified to forgive human lies?

We can be part of Christmas all year
if we invite Him into our lives—
then all year long we'll know the Glory,
Peace and Hope where Salvation abides!

As We Study an Old Photograph . . .

David Black

(First place, poetry, Blue Ridge Writers Contest, VWC; first place
State VWC Golden Nib Contest. 2019)

Here's Josh, about age three, on the sidewalk
and a dog standing behind him, staring
to the side at something we cannot see.
Big and brown, he strongly favors Jackson,
Josh's old chow mix that still lives with us,
but the photo goes back some thirty years—
and here is a different pet, and we three,
try as we will, cannot remember him
at all.
      Josh half-jokes that he's owned him twice,
this forgotten friend caught in a time warp
from his youth. I tell myself he's a ghost,
like the Civil War soldier who shows up
in a black-and-white with one's grandparents
from 1933 . . . a strange woman
seen in the background of last year's photo
of smiling newlyweds . . .
              tales heard often
enough to make us ask how this could be,
what there is in and out of this world that
we cannot fully know, curious if
we leave here some whisper of our presence
that lingers and disturbs the order that
people think they know, just as we, from time
to time feel the return of family,
friend, or creaky old pet so strongly that
we weep—and sad that without the picture
to hand to you, we will not be believed.

All Hallows' Eve

David Black

Here begins the half-year of death
when the Veil is thin and the Other World is nigh,
the blessed dead slip through,
and revenants and witches visit
kirkyards, moors, and homes,

where they are frightened off by torch and candle,
by bonfires scattered across glen and brae—
eighty such counted from a single tor—
lit to rid each farm of nighthags and warlocks
and fight the ascendant dark.

But the shades have now lost their power
and little guisers don't fear the baneful dead.
They mimic ghoulies and ghosties,
prank their way around our towns,
and plead for little bribes.

Tubs of bobbing apples remind us
that the Silver Bough of Avalon
lies somewhere just beyond the sacred waters,
and witch-consuming fires live only
in hollow pumpkin shells.

Our riderless cats arch their paper backs
and never mew, Auld Nick
finds a gap-toothed princess in his place,
and a slivered candy moon
does little to replace the dying sun.

There's no sense of primal threat,
nor cleansing of crofters' field by bonfires
and torchlit marches along their bounds—
no solemn rite here to ease the heart and blood,
to say that death is overcome.

PROSE NONFICTION

She had stopped eating and drinking, a sign the body is shutting down. A week, they say, is about as long as one can expect.

Again my brother and I flew in from our separate cities, met and drove to our hometown.

We arrived mid morning and hoped we would be in time.

The small room was quiet. My small mother lay in her bed, white sheets and white blanket to tuck her in. Her skin was still beautiful, her face and hands lovely. When I held her hand, I saw it was the same size and shape as mine.

They had let her hair grow long and put it in one braid at the back. She would not have liked that, I think. In my memories of her, she always wore it fairly short and nicely done. But I suppose this was easier to care for. It made her look so young, like in her pictures from high school and college.

I leaned close and put my cheek to hers, told her who I was, that I was here, that I loved her. At the sound of my name, her eyelids fluttered, and I knew that she knew. She also knew my brother was here. She had been holding on until we came.

At that point, the process of a long life began in earnest to move through its final duties, each part ending. She had been cool to the touch when I arrived. Now, in the afternoon, she grew warm, cheeks slightly flushed, her breathing more rapid. Not a struggle, just that last quickening, all rather gentle and polite, no fuss, the way she had always been.

My mother's best friend slipped into the room just before it happened, as if she knew when the time would be, the one who drove my mother to all the writers' conferences and speaking engagements in her last years. We held a mirror and found no sign of breath.

My brother looked at his watch. Three, exactly. He called the others to let them know. We waited for the ones to arrive who would take her away.

Later, as we cleaned out the cabinets and drawers of the room, removed pictures from the wall, I noticed the clock that hung there. All those last years whenever I visited, it had been stopped at three. No one bothered to fix it, and my mother was unable to see.

I needed to tell her about the clock and the stopped hour. She would enjoy it. We would talk and develop the idea. We were excited together about words and thoughts like this, making phone calls, writing letters constantly, sending drafts for critique. I would have no one now to talk to about such things.

I have trouble saying the word "died" in connection with my mother. I have trouble with the word "death." The sound of it leaves silence and an empty space after it is spoken. That is how I felt as we made preparations. Everyone carefully used other ways of saying it. But it could not be avoided. The word hollowed me out.

My mother in her thoughtfulness had planned everything beforehand. But there were still things to be decided. I sat in the office of the funeral director. Then I would look at the hands in my lap, my hand reaching for a paper he gave me, and it was my mother's hand. In my voice was her voice. She was in the gestures and words and postures of my brother and sister.

She had chosen for herself the same style of casket as for my father at his burial, but this had been discontinued. Here were the new and nearest equivalents, and we must decide the color preferred.

They looked at me. I was the one who thought like her. I chose the palest bronze, the paler fittings, the pale color of tea seen within a white porcelain cup, the surface polished like glass. I thought of Sappho and her spare, dignified poems, the coffin like a beautiful ode.

He set a calendar before us to plan the funeral date. Now, for the first time, I saw it. The day she died is the second day of February.

I wanted to tell my brother and sister, point out the significance, but am not yet sure if I will cry or laugh, or both. I cannot trust myself.

Groundhog Day. Candlemas. The Feast of the Presentation. Three o'clock. I am held in a tale, the plot so neatly conceived so it is easy to remember. My father would have made much of the conjunction of events. He would humorously pronounce it a Day of Destiny, as he did for occasions of note.

At the wake, I approached her as she lay in the lovely sapphic ode I had chosen for her, the pale bronze now pinkish in

136

soft lighting. Her hair had been trimmed and curled just as it used to be. Her hands felt like marble.

At the funeral, we three grown children sat in the first pew with the casket before us. My brother leaned to us and said, "We move up a row now."

Our parents and all the older ones were gone, and, along with them, our status as children. It was our turn to be the grown-ups.

Funerals are strange occasions. They hurt so much, but I know they are necessary. They allow us to resolve. They allow us to bring memories together in a way that we can select and hold. The minister, a good friend of hers and someone who knows literature, read Dickinson's poem, "Because I could not stop for Death," and I just about lost it. Tissues were handed to me from both sides.

But the poem was to become a comfort. As he read it, I saw her sitting on the seat of the carriage beside Death. They talked as they rode. She had that long braid again. She was a girl. My mother would make a friend even here. She would find out his history, that she knew his cousin, and remember the experience for a poem she might write.

I imagined her, a silhouette in the carriage, proceeding the funeral cars. We moved in slow procession through the streets of the town and to the cemetery where she would lie beside my father, her mother and father and brother, and her grandson.

It was winter, but a bright day. The casket rested on its platform, dark evergreens all around the clearing. We took our places. We heard the words. I watched the sun linger and gleam on the pale polished bronze, the paler fittings, like flame carried home to light a house, a day of sun strong enough for a groundhog to see its shadow, depending on where he stood. Perhaps more weeks of winter, but then spring, always spring.

It has been six years, and every year it hurts the same when I lift the calendar page and find the day that used to be just a part of folklore and history. Now my mother is also within that small, innocent number in the small square on the page.

For some reason I especially dreaded facing it this year. I felt ill the night before. On February 2, I told myself I had to get through this until three o'clock. I would carry her along with me and think of her, and I did. Then, just after three, the darkness of my grief fell away.

I found myself suddenly laughing as I thought of one of her poems. My mother published twenty books at least, most of them poetry. She was poet laureate of our state, recipient of awards and accolades, subject of interviews, sought-after for readings and teachings. Writing was her life, and life was the material for her writing. She proclaimed it everywhere. She saw connections in everything and wrote about it.

I will have to suppose her exit at the figure of three on the clock and two on the calendar, the day of groundhog and candles, was a way to reach me, because she knew I would see the connection, and I would think of it each time it came around. Remember this, she might say. Use it. Write about it. It's important. Everything is important.

The poem I am thinking of concerns her visit to Dove Cottage, the house of Wordsworth, in the Lake District. A small chair has a sign cautioning not to sit. But, of course, one woman cannot resist. She is too heavy, far too large, but she giggles coyly and lowers herself in a pose before the guide spots her.

"Do I dare, and will I fit?" is the line my mother says of the woman.

When I find the poem and reread it, I am surprised not to see this quote. I realize it is one of her comments to us or in a presentation about her poetry, and now part of our family lore. We often say it when deciding a course of action.

I laugh to think of it. And now I laugh again as I imagine my slender mother, her youthful self, climb into the carriage, look around at me, smile and say, in that distinct enunciation, "Do I dare, and will I fit?"

And she does. She settles down beside her friend, and off they go, to the slant rhyme and rhythm of Emily's piece, all the way back through the number on the calendar that holds marmots, candles, and old tales, light all around them, the brightening of the year.

O Christmas Tree

Deborah Prum

(Second place, nonfiction, *Skyline* Winter Holidays Contest, 2019)

Our first Christmas tree was a pine branch stuck into a white plastic milk jug. That year, we'd been married for only two months when I came down with meningitis in mid-November. Distracted by my potential imminent demise, my husband, Bruce, did not attempt to decorate. So, on Christmas Eve, a friend of ours kindly left the branch in a jug on our doorstep.

During the next few years of married life, we lived in an apartment so small you could use a short-corded vacuum to clean the whole place without ever having to shift to a second outlet. Our miniscule living room had space for a couch, a coffee table and standing room for one person, one skinny person. So, there wasn't a single spot to squeeze in a Christmas tree. Instead, we hung three shiny red orbs on a ficus plant nicknamed Spike.

Later, we moved to North Carolina, where we lived in a tiny rented house and lived on an even tinier student budget. Our sons (five and three) danced with glee when we told them we'd planned to spring for a real Christmas tree. Bruce brought home a Scotch pine. About two minutes after hanging our meager ornaments, one member of our family, who shall remain nameless, experienced an overwhelming asthma attack. We wound up giving the tree, decorations and all, to a neighbor. In exchange, she sent over her two-foot high, PINK, aluminum tree that my little boys greeted with great wailing and gnashing of teeth.

From then on, we Prums wisely purchased Douglas Firs—trees our sensitive lungs could handle. However, all those years of Christmas Decoration Deprivation took its toll on my husband's psyche. Now, the day after Thanksgiving, he goes into a festooning frenzy, draping every square inch of our house with holiday doodads. Our home looks like the set from *Sanford and Son*—for you youngsters, it was a seventies TV show that takes place in a junkyard.

My sentimental husband has saved every last Christmas craft our non-artistically gifted children have produced, the most memorable of which is a crèche. When the boys were in elementary school, they went through a short-lived carpentry phase. They constructed a crèche composed of sawed-off tops of two-by-fours, each standing about six inches high. With magic markers, the boys drew figures on the boards: wise men, wise sheep, a donkey, shepherds, a possible space alien, Joseph, the baby Jesus, and so forth. Unfortunately, the marker ink bled into the grain of the wood, producing a surrealistic visual effect, notably on the Virgin Mary's face, which, suffice it to say, does *not* look beatific.

Not only are our decorations aesthetically underwhelming, but some are also dangerous, namely an ornament I've dubbed *The Killer Angel.* Designed by a maniacal kindergarten teacher, it's constructed entirely from tin can parts. The sharp wings could easily slice off a finger. I'm not even exaggerating. Oh, maybe I'm exaggerating a little.

Now that the kids are adults, when Christmas rolls around, they don't always make it back for the holidays. Although I've been cranky about our tasteless decorations, I'll have to admit, I'm grateful for the little reminders of the children displayed throughout the house. And now--don't tell Bruce this—with three grandchildren in the mix, I'm looking forward to new craft projects hanging from the limbs of our very full tree.

Dear Santa

Deborah Prum

As you might remember, when I was seven, all I wanted for Christmas was a live horse and a real gun. I envisioned myself patrolling our neighborhood, on the lookout for bad guys. I didn't intend to shoot the bad guys, only brandish my firearm, telling them, "Stop picking on the little guys. Be good, *or else.*"

And Santa, you know we did have some actual bad guys in our neighborhood, two gangs similar to the Sharks and Jets, but our gangs called themselves The Earls and The Lords. They sounded like British royalty instead of the petty criminals that they were. I'm guessing those bad guys routinely wound up at the top of your Naughty List. To be honest, the Earls and Lords bothered other adults, not us. So, the bad boys I was after were the ones on the playground who knocked us off of our bikes and gave killer wedgies.

Back to the horse. You're probably wondering where I planned to keep the animal, since I lived in a brick apartment building with asphalt behind and concrete out front. Neither place offered much in the way of grazing. The horse could have nibbled on the tiny square of grass by the front stoop, but that "hardly would have filled his eye tooth," as my Italian relatives like to say.

And, how about that gun? How likely were my parents to allow me to ride around pointing a gun at people? My folks came from a long line of pacifists. Moreover, they were not the kind of crazy people who would consider arming a small child. Did I let those facts stop me from requesting a gun and horse each year?

Ever the optimist, I'd peer out my bedroom window on Christmas morning, expecting to see a horse tethered to the doorknob of my father's little upholstery shop. Santa, you never delivered the live horse and the real gun. Instead, I'd find one of my father's white tube socks filled with onions and small change. To be fair, other presents sat under the tree, which soon made me forget about the lack of a live horse.

When I was about ten, I gave up on you. I realized there was no way you could fit down the stovepipe of our gas range.

141

Yet, that year a medium-sized box with my name on it arrived under the tree before Christmas. Could it be a gun? Dare I hope?

Turned out, my grandfather had given me a Rainbow children's Bible, the one with Jesus on the cover, peacefully sitting on a rock, teaching a large group of children who also look quite peaceful (and a little Swedish—fair skin, blond hair, blue eyes). So, my gift was a Bible, not the gun for which I'd pined. Even at that tender age, the irony was not lost on me.

As disappointed as I was to receive the Bible, I'll concede that the "Love your enemies" style of relating to people advocated in the book of Matthew is a better way to deal with folks than my "Hands up! Behave or else!" method of crowd control.

However, the cover on that Rainbow Bible still gives me pause. Why would all those pale Swedish kids be sitting around Jesus right in the middle of the burning hot desert? They're not wearing hats and likely did not apply sunscreen. It just doesn't make sense.

Regardless, at a time where there's not much of either, here's to peace on earth and goodwill toward men. Happy holidays, Santa!

Lots of love and I really mean it.

Taking the Plunge

Susan M. Lanterman

(Third place, nonfiction, *Skyline* Winter Holidays Contest, 2019)

Getting married was not *my* idea. After five years of an "on again, off again" courtship, we flipped a coin to see whether my mother would win the toss and host the wedding of *her* dreams for her only daughter.

Brian's relationship with my parents was awkward at best. He had been a rascal during high school. Though a perpetual underachiever academically, he excelled in rabble rousing and good-natured silliness. I was a moth to his flame, as they say. My parents were underwhelmed with my choice.

Our adventure began when I found a note rolled up like a "cigarette" tucked (i.e., visibly propped) in the pocket of my suede purse. Smoking was an offense of the highest order at St. Mary's High School. This got my attention—as I had never partaken of the deadly sin of smoking.

"I've been watching you for a while," the note said. The scribbled handwriting was unremarkable: its author could be a sociopath for all I knew. "If you're interested in meeting up sometime, you will know it's me by my pink tie." This was clearly a joke.

I interrogated my best friends, but no one 'fessed up. After I glared down every hall at school for days, Brian finally appeared in the last row of Junior English, with a boyish grin and a hot pink tie. It was love at first sight.

Agile and athletic, he consistently maintained a grade-point average that would barely allow him to participate in soccer and baseball. Brian lacked the bravado of his teammates. Choosing to wear his lucky number "13," he was the anomaly on both teams. He warmed the bench until there was a clutch moment when brains overruled brawn. Then, just like Clark Kent, he would toss aside his dry, scratchy security towel hanging around his neck and race onto the field to pull off a killer pitch or a gritty goal. I observed this as I did all sports—as a bored spectator.

The coaches at St. Mary's were very conservative. One was known as "The Drill-Sergeant" because he had been in the Marines. Brian's shaggy blond hair was an offense to both team coaches—especially when it flipped-off Coach Marshall by protruding from the back of his baseball cap. I accompanied Brian to the barbershop, where he had his ponytail cut off. He put it in a rectangular box with "R.I.P." inscribed on the lid and left it on the coach's desk the next day. At the end of a dismal season, Brian felt a certain bond with his position on the bench, so he took a saw to his seat and made it into a footstool in shop class.

As the second child in my family, I stood in awe of my often "disrespectful" and outrageously behaved brother. While I greatly appreciated his audacity, I merely tiptoed through the ashes of the trails he blazed. When Brian would wait for me nervously on our front lawn, Joe barely acknowledged him, with a nod. Joe emitted testosterone in a force field that no one dared invade or even approach. He was a star basketball player at the local college—and you know what happens if you get too close to a star.

My parents expressed no opinion about Brian to me, except that they were glad he was "seeing" their daughter (who had previously vowed to have no boyfriends before him and had envisioned living alone the rest of her life). Being my brother's sister, I was taught to play "Horse" as a child, only so he could beat me at hoops. I wore a tattered "Real Girls Drive Sticks" T-shirt as an emblem of my superiority—plus to keep the boys at bay.

After a few months of mutual adoration, Brian surprised me by kneeling at one of the baseball games and asking me to the senior prom. "How ceremonial of you!" I responded with a sweaty blush. My father was a prankster, so I lived in expectation of the unexpected.

"You *do* know that Brian must ask me for permission to take you to the ball." My father was a stickler for "pomp and circumstance." Up until then, Brian had mostly avoided conversing with my family. "I'm Cinderella, for God's sake," I complained. "I wanted to sneak out after dark and return before dawn. I'm lucky to even have a date, and now you want to ruin it!"

"At the very least there will be no sneaking out. He must be properly ID'd and photographed before departing with you for said ball." The upshot was that we would be forced to present ourselves before the talking head of my family—plus my mother, who was the real ruler.

Brian was a walking contradiction: both painfully shy and ridiculously comical. On prom night he showed up at the door in a white tux with black trim and naturally . . . in a hot pink, frilly shirt. After my mother had insisted dress shopping with me (and proposed a dozen candidates in various colors of the rainbow), I had ultimately chosen a black gown. "You look pretty enough for the two of us," I whispered in Brian's ear, walking toward the family room.

As we approached, my father was sitting in his lounge chair, with his back to us. Just as I noticed the butt end of the antique shotgun, which normally hung on the mantle, he twirled around and hoisted it upright. "You wanna to take good care of my little gal Suzy here," he pronounced, with a fake drawl. "If you break her heart, I might just need to perform a shotgun wedding."

"Oh, just shoot me now!" I retorted, cringing.

"I'll get my camera and it'll all be over in just a minute," Dad hurriedly replied.

Our senior year of high school was a blur of sporting events, concerts, finals, and anxiety. Brian was heading to school in Florida, where he could traverse athletic fields year-round, whilst I was attending college in my own backyard. We knew it would be impossible to carry on a long-distance alliance with all of the inevitable distractions.

Fast-forward four years and a few dalliances later. I caught sight of Brian leaning awkwardly on the perimeter of a reunion/Christmas party in our hometown. My heart thumped and we resumed our allegiance to each other. In a matter of months, we completed our obligation to fulfill our parents' aspirations for our college educations and looked forward to a new-found independence.

"Wouldn't it be nice if we were older / Then we wouldn't have to wait so long…" I sang the Beach Boys' lyrics to Brian. We began searching for a city to move to so we could be "Happy Together."

Then my father reappeared, brandishing that imaginary firearm. He popped the question of marriage to Brian. "You never succumbed to peer pressure before this," I poked Brian, "so why the paternal pressure now?"

"I don't know . . . . It's just when he looks up at me with those doe-like eyes and says 'why live together, why not get married?' I've got nothing to say. I'm not opposed to being conventional. Do you want to?"

I wasn't averse to the idea. Dating other people had only convinced me that it was either Brian or going back to solitary confinement. But I just couldn't concede to my parents' demands without a preparatory skirmish. Previously, my mother had remained on the sidelines. Now she was joining forces with my father—making them the dynamic duo of unrelenting reasoning and shame.

"What would your grandmother think about you living in sin?"

"You mean if she were still alive?"

"She would turn in her grave!" My mother evoked the name of my dearly departed grandmother whenever she needed to lower the boom. Like the Ghost of Christmas Past, Grandma's specter was summoned to loom over my random decisions and add an ominous shroud of doom.

"I don't want a wedding. What if Brian and I just elope?" My mother's face turned crimson. The only family member to elope had been my aunt Shirley, and that marriage had not gone well. Shirley was Annette Funicello to my ex-uncle Luke's embodiment of Elvis Presley. For all of the Lucky Strikes rolled up in his sleeve, he turned out to be "nothin' but a hound dog." To even mention eloping was tantamount to cursing our union outright.

I gave in, saying I would allow my parents to invite fifty of their "closest friends" to a low-key celebration of our nuptials. Well, the guest list quickly ballooned to 100. While Brian basked in the light of parental acceptance for proposing, I passively aggressively resisted every step of the wedding planning process.

"What do you want for flowers?" my mother cooed.

"Black-eyed Susans."

"How about having your cousin Lori sing?" she suggested.

146

"How about Lori sings 'The Sound of Silence?'" I replied.

My mother pitched ideas; I batted them out of the park. Her pièce de résistance was the bridal gown.

"Do you want 'something old or something new'?" Mom asked, coyly.

"Blue—definitely blue. As in blue jeans," I quipped.

Her scream could be heard around the block.

Dad came in as the relief pitcher. "Look, try to work with your mother on this wedding thing. She never got to plan her own wedding, so this will be her only chance . . . . Unless *you* have a daughter, and I live long enough to experience this nightmare all over again!"

"You're so small boned," Mom coaxed. "Why don't you try on Grandma's lovely gown? It never fit me because I'm built like an ox—like your grandfather—*may he rest in peace.* But it's bound to fit you."

For as long as I could remember, Grandma's wedding gown had hung in the hall closet, entombed in a heavy plastic garment bag. Mom was correct. When I had last snuck into the sanctum sanctorum at age twelve and tried it on, it had fit. My girlfriend Cherry had helped me secure all fifty satin buttons up the back. In her wedding album, Grandma looked like a mermaid with a satin fin. Although we weren't supposed to play dress up in the gown, I was enticed by it (like Eve in the Garden of Eden), and I had to try it on—just once.

"I don't think I'm interested in the 'something old' department," I announced. "I'll buy a dress before the wedding."

"That's what I'm afraid of," Mom moaned.

However, as the big day approached, I began to panic about my attire. Cherry was my "Best Woman," (never to be referred to as "The Old Maid of Honor") so she accompanied me on a secret trip to a bridal shop. It was where one of those dog-and-pony shows occurs: everyone sits in a circle and critiques the bride's choices until she starts crying and picks what *they've* voted for. Armed with a blank check from the father of the bride, I found an affordable dress that could have doubled as a tent. No lace, no frills, and plenty of room for comfort. It was—as Goldilocks said—"just right."

"I'll take one like this; it's a size 6. Can it be shipped to my friend?" (I wasn't taking any chances that my mother would infiltrate my decision.)

All systems were *go* for the bride and groom's launch into marital bliss. The gown had arrived on time, and Cherry's mom had even steamed it for me.

"Don't you want to play dress up again and try your wedding dress on?" Cherry was clearly more excited than me. "No, isn't it bad luck for you to see me in my gown before the wedding?" Traditions of any type puzzled her. Every day my mother chanted, "When can I see your gown?" And every time I echoed back, "on my wedding day."

Finally, the time had come to seal the deal. Traditionally, our family arrived just seconds before other people's weddings began. Once my father actually set a pick, throwing out an arm to block the bride before she walked down the aisle so we could all "sneak" in first. As my mother was wont to grumble, she seethed, "Your father will be late to his own funeral."

Now it was our time to be fashionably late. I purposely sat in the kitchen snacking while everyone swirled around me, finding things to worry about.

"How come *you* get to eat before the reception?" my brother pouted.

"Because it's *my* wedding. And everyone says the bride and groom never have time to eat. Besides, I have lots of room in my wedding gown for a full tummy."

I realized it was just about time for Cherry to triumphantly escort the dress over from her house, as the wedding ceremony was about an hour off. A few minutes later, she walked into my room carrying what looked like a body bag. She was already dressed, with her makeup perfectly applied and her hair strategically coiffed atop her head.

"Wow! You sure are tiny!" she said, taking the gown out and holding it up to herself.

"That doesn't look like the pup tent I chose," I replied, nervously.

"The tag says size 6" Cherry declared, unzipping the dress.

Sweat began to materialize under each arm. Cherry lifted the fabric over my shoulders and gazed at the crevasse created by the open zipper. She let out a shriek.

"This dress is the wrong size! It's got to be a 4 or maybe even a 2!"

I turned to look at my back in the full-length mirror and gasped for air.

"No, no, no!" I shouted. "The label said 6!"

My mother flew into the room, with her own dress unzipped.

"What happened? What's wrong?" Observing the garment gaping open on my back, she held her manicured hand to her mouth and uttered something unintelligible.

"Do you have one of those shawls that Grandma used to wear? I said, in a voice that sounded calm, albeit shaky. One that looks like a big triangle?"

"NO, NO, NO!" she shouted. "I *knew* something bad was bound to happen!"

I flopped on the bed and began to regret my cavalier attitude about the whole wedding day business. "Think fast, think fast . . ." I told no one in particular. If only l liked dressing up and had a plethora of choices in my closet. "Do you have any dresses that would fit me?" I asked Cherry, who was at least three sizes bigger.

"Never mind. How about your mother? She's short. Doesn't she have one of those Mumu dresses from Hawaii?" Sighing, my mother collapsed on the bed next to me and proclaimed, "This is an utter disaster."

I had hoped to avoid the family curse by not eloping, but Grandma was getting the last laugh after all. Grandma . . . .

I sat upright with my forefinger pointing towards the sky, like I had just made a slam dunk for the team. "Mom, you were right all along!"

Sixty minutes later (more or less), I was standing arm in arm with my sweaty dad. A bouquet of black-eyed Susans and hot pink roses gripped tightly in my hands. All fifty satin buttons were present and accounted for as I walked ever so carefully down the aisle, trying not to step on the "fin" of my grandmother's satin gown.

149

Winter, What Is It Like?

Stephen Bush

In Australia what winter is like varies; in Spain it varies even more. I made the change and now I could have a day of snow in winter, something not possible in any of the places I lived in Australia. But in summer in Galicia, in the Ribeira Sacra, it will be in the 30s, or should I say, in Fahrenheit, from the mid 80s to the mid 90s, with cool nights. In Australia it tended to stay hot at night if it was a hot day, but not here.

Winter starts in earnest in late October in Galicia. The days can still be warm enough for swimming in the Minho River during the first week or two of October, but by now the fires will be lit at night to keep the house warm. It is past the time to make sure you have a good supply of wood and to make sure there is enough gasoil in the tank if you have central heating running on that.

If you are an organized person with land with trees growing on it, preferably Spanish oak trees, they burn the hottest and longest, you will have cut your wood and brought it home and put it in the barn in May or even April. You will have time in those months for woodcutting and carting and stacking before you need to start working on your grapevines and on your huerta, your vegetable garden.

The Ribeira Sacra is a place of definite seasons, unlike most of Australia, where they tend to gradually arrive, and definitely not like Northern Australia, where it is always hot and the only variation is if it is raining daily or not raining at all—the Wet Season and the Dry Season, as they are known. There are no such things as autumn and spring there.

The native pine forests on the steep river banks of the Sil and Minho rivers in the Ribeira Sacra are green all year, but the Spanish oaks and most other trees shed their leaves in autumn in a brief display of restrained color. The occasional patches of American oaks are an exception, their dying leaves being bright red. The Spanish oaks are far more bland. The grasses die off and things are quiet on the huerta, with the last produce picked by late

151

October or occasionally early November. I have picked the last green tomatoes that late. Down in the river valleys of the Minho and Sil things grow for longer than they do higher up where it is cooler and windier.

Winter arrives gently and is coldest in late January and in February, but when we had a big snowfall here a couple of years ago it was in March. Winter likes to jump up and surprise you just when you think it is starting to leave. The snow started falling in the very early hours and fell on into the morning. It didn't sit for long, though. It was over a foot deep on the ground when it stopped falling and had mostly disappeared within twenty-four hours. Apparently, thirty or forty years ago there was a big snowfall in the village and people were trapped here for a week, but that was before everyone had a car and the road was worse.

The snow fell too early to affect the grapes. But that year was also a wet year and that did affect them. The grapes grown in the thousands of small terraced vineyards rising up from the rivers Minho and Sil, the home of what is proudly called "Heroic" viticulture, are the most important thing in the lives of many people in the Ribeira Sacra. Ribeira Sacra means Sacred Riverbank and the name comes from the middle ages when there were numerous monasteries along the river.

Years before the monasteries the Romans lived here and mined gold and made wine. This is a rich region. The Minho and the Sil rivers join together at Os Peares, and the Minho continues to the Atlantic and, on the last part of its journey, provides the border between Portugal and Spain. There it runs between the wonderfully preserved heavily fortified towns of Tui on the Spanish side and Valenca on the Portuguese side.

Os Peares is now the home of one of the many small-to-medium-sized hydroelectric dams built by Spanish dictator Francisco Franco along these two rivers. Before the dams were built in the 1960s there was no bitumen road linking the villages along the Minho, only a dirt one dating from ancient times, and the rivers provided the transport to take the wine to the bigger cities along the riverbanks. The rivers were also full of salmon and trout, now long gone and replaced by black bass, a destructive fish from the United States.

In summer the roads in the Ribeira Sacra are almost bustling with tourists and people tending their vineyards, building to a crescendo of tourists in August and then in late September or early October to a plethora of vineyard workers here for the grape harvest, Vendimia. Now roads that are usually deserted see large trucks arrive to take away the grapes picked by hand on numerous small vineyards and carried up to the road in cubos, plastic containers, by hardy locals, many in their sixties and seventies, the "Heroic" viticulture. On the Sil there are vineyards where the grapes go on boats to the bodegas, as there is no other way to get to the grapes.

But in winter the Ribeira Sacra is left to the people living here who can enjoy having empty roads again, taking holidays while there is no work to do, or just relaxing by the "economo" in the kitchen. This cast-iron wood-fired cooking stove, built with bricks and cast-iron pieces, is still found in most village kitchens, including mine, and was often formerly built in the center of the room, like an island, with a wooden bench along the back of it to sit on to keep warm. The parts are still made in Spain and can be bought new for installation in your kitchen. Or maybe they sit by one of the modern versions of a wood-cooking stove used for central heating, like a friend of mine has.

It is not so many years ago that winter meant sitting almost on top of the small cooking fire burning on a stone hearth at one side of the small room used for preparing food. These can still be seen in many old houses. It was a much colder life back then unless you had a good number of cows or sheep living in the barn under your floor that were providing lots of extra heat to your house.

The best things about winter here are the peace and quiet of having few people about; the clean air, which is so pure that even going to the local village can seem like going into a cloud of noxious pollution; the magical views; and the wildlife.

There is definitely a lot of good to a winter life in the Ribeira Sacra region of Galicia.

A Monterey Christmas

Gary D. Kessler

"Look at that sunshine. Another beautiful Monterey morning."

Yes, it certainly was, I thought, my face set in such a grim line that Dad gave me a perplexed look. The weather report the previous night had talked about a cold snap, and I had bounced out of bed early that morning and rushed to the door, so sure that, although it almost was coming too late, the white Christmas I had known previously at our Denver house had finally reached us on the California coast.

"No snow." The statement was curt and tense; the words clipped.

"Of course not, silly," said Dad. "It's cooler than yesterday, but it's still a balmy 70 degrees." Dad took a deep breath and smiled up at the sky. "Have you ever seen such a glorious day?"

Obviously, I had—but not like this monotonously warm weather. Glorious to me at Christmas time was like when it snowed for Christmas in Colorado. I sank down on the step up to the front porch and buried my chin in my fists. Dad just didn't understand. The lack of snow was just a symbol of everything gone wrong.

At last Dad caught on, and he sat down on the step beside me. "Listen, big guy, you know we moved here because we learned those Colorado winters were bad for your condition. Christmas comes to California just like it comes to Colorado, you know. Christmas isn't about the weather—at least not much."

I moved ever so slightly away from him. It figured that this was all my fault, that there was no snow because they had to bring me here. "Does not; in Colorado Christmas comes with snow."

A long pause. Dad nudged me playfully with an elbow, but I wasn't having any of that today. With an audible sigh, Dad stood up. "Well, times a wastin', and we have things to do." He yelled back toward the open front door, "Mom, need some soap flakes, matches, and food coloring. Think you can rustle those up for us?"

I knew Dad was just trying to catch my attention, and I sank my chin deeper into my hands and hunched my shoulders. Life was the pits. Nothing had been right since we moved here.

Dad moved toward the door. "Well, you gonna' come in and help?"

A long pause. "Can't. Told Jimmy I'd bike over to his place this morning."

Dad gave me a sharp look and almost said something. But then he just shrugged his shoulders and walked into the house.

My mood only darkened further when I arrived at Jimmy's. Jimmy and his mom were bustling around, packing suitcases, and chattering with excitement. A happy family.

"What's up?" I asked Jimmy.

"Mom and I are going up into the mountains for Christmas," Jimmy answered. His eyes were dancing with joy.

Up into the mountains. Snow. I couldn't help it; the frustration was too much. I'd wanted Dad to fight with me on this—to help me feel it wasn't my fault we weren't having a white Christmas. We were in Monterey because the doctors told my parents they needed to get me in the sunshine. So, this was all my fault. Tears formed in my eyes. I was so homesick for the Colorado life we'd left behind—my cousins and all my friends.

"That's . . . that's great," I finally managed to get out. "Your dad going too?"

"Naw," Jimmy responded with a slight frown. "He says he don't like the cold and snow and has a golfin' game to go to here on Christmas Eve. He and Mom aren't talkin' . . . again."

"Oh, that's too bad," I said. But what was really too bad was that Jimmy was going to get to go to the mountains and have a white Christmas and I wasn't. And suddenly that was just too much to bear. I jumped back on my bicycle and managed a "Have a great time," before I wheeled off. But, when I was well out of hearing, I couldn't help finishing it off with the self-pitying, "I sure wish it was me."

Just before that, though, I turned and looked back at Jimmy. I was already out of his mind; his mom had come out on

156

their porch and was leaning down and listening to whatever Jimmy was saying to her.

I was fighting the bile of resentment as I reached home, but that battle was being lost. Jimmy was my best friend, but why did Jimmy have all the luck? Why did Jimmy's parents love him so much that he could go to snow for Christmas? Why had everyone else gotten all of the good parents who understood and did something about it?

As I entered the house, I heard my dad off in the dining room. He was whistling the "White Christmas" song, and I almost burst into tears on the spot. That was just rubbing it in. Probably Dad's way of punishing me for being so crabby with him. The music drew me to the dining room, however, and there were my dad and mom—and something I had never seen before.

Dad had taken down the big mirror over the buffet and had it leaning up against some boxes on the dining room table. Mom was standing in the doorway to the kitchen, pouring Ivory Snow flakes into a bowl and whipping up what must have been a second or third batch of fluffy white soap suds. They foamed up to look just like . . . snow.

Dad had just about finished making a picture on the mirror. When he saw me enter the room, he gathered me in with an arm and started pointing out the features of the Christmas mural he had created. The mountains that had been made out of white soap suds enclosed a miniature valley with log houses made out of matchsticks, pine trees made with dyed soap suds, and an area left open to the mirror surface that looked just like a frozen lake. One matchstick man was skiing down a mountain and another was skating on the pond.

I gasped in recognition. This looked just like my grandmom's Colorado mountain valley at Christmas time. The picture was beautiful. I never knew my dad could make something so beautiful. And he had done it just for me.

Mom, Dad, and I sat around the dining room table, murmuring to each other and laughing at the occasional joke as Dad put the finishing touches on the Christmas picture. The phone rang, and Mom told me it was for me.

"Hi, this is Jimmy. My mom wants to know if you want to go to the mountains with us this Christmas. Can you? I know it would be fun."

I was nearly speechless. "Uh, thanks Jimmy. I mean . . . really thanks. That would be wonderful . . . and I really, really appreciate you asking . . . but my dad has asked me to help him with something tomorrow, and I really gotta stay here and do it."

The next day, Jimmy and his mom waved from their car as they passed the house on their way to the mountains. Jimmy's dad wasn't in the car, but then I didn't expect to see him there. At the familiar honk of the horn, I and my parents rushed to the window—now laced with soap suds snowflakes—and waved back enthusiastically. Then we returned to spreading whipped Ivory Snow soapsuds into the shape of snowflakes and drifting snow on the other windows of our California bungalow under the warm Monterey sun.

Coach Daniel

Gerry Kruger

(Third place, nonfiction, Blue Ridge Writers Chapter Contest, VWC, 2018)

April 2017, Charlottesville, Virginia

Getting home from running errands is the balm for my aching feet and tired eyes. I balance a bag of groceries on one arm and manage to unlock my front door. As soon as I step inside, the phone rings. "COLTON" appears on the Caller ID. Could it be Wayne Colton from Spotsylvania County? Why would he be calling me?

I set the groceries on the kitchen counter and pick up the receiver of the wall phone just above it. "Hello?"

"Hello, this is Wayne Colton," a pleasant male voice answers. "I'm a friend of your father. Is this Gerry?"

"Yes." I glance at my bag of groceries and think about the ice cream melting, but I want to know why Wayne Colton is calling. "Didn't my dad and I see you last year at Bonefish Grill?"

"That's right."

"You came to our table to speak to us."

"Yes."

"Daddy was so pleased to see you."

"Actually, I'm calling about your dad. Your brother told me you were writing a book about him."

"Yes, I visit him every week in Fredericksburg and we work on the book." I take the ice cream out of the grocery bag. It needs to go into the freezer.

Wayne continues, "If you have a minute, I'd like to tell you a story about him that happened when I was growing up."

"Thanks, that would be great. Let me get something to write with. Just a minute."

What a surprise! A story about my dad. I manage to put the ice cream in the freezer. The rest of the groceries can wait. I take a deep breath and grab a ballpoint pen and notepad from beneath the phone. "I'm putting you on speaker phone. Okay?"

"Sure. I think this story shows a lot about the kind of man your father is."

1947, Spotsylvania, Virginia

"What time is your baseball game today, son?" Harry Colton noticed his nine-year-old boy looking down at his unfinished bowl of oatmeal.

Wayne swallowed and mumbled, "Five o'clock." Why would he need to know? Since he had joined the neighborhood team two years ago, his father had never attended a single one of his games. Everyone else's parents came to some of their games, but his dad always said he couldn't leave work.

Wayne poked at his oatmeal with his spoon. He doubted that his father had any idea how important baseball was to him. He dreamed of one day becoming a professional baseball player. Mr. Daniel, one of the coaches, had talked to him about practicing and working hard. He said he was a good athlete and had potential. Sometimes he wished Mr. Daniel was his dad. The boy's blue-green eyes brimmed with tears. He wiped them away with his napkin so his mother wouldn't see as she picked up some dishes and took them to the kitchen sink to wash.

"I think I can get off early today and make it to your game."

Wayne's head snapped back, his eyes wide as he eyed his father standing behind him. "Really? You're coming to my game?"

"The boss said he could do without me this time." Wayne's dad smiled down at the face that looked up at him.

The boy bounced out of his chair and wrapped both arms around the towering figure. Wayne was growing taller almost every day. He might even grow to be taller than his dad. Mr. Daniel said his height would be an asset to the game.

"Thanks, Dad." He could hardly choke out the words. His dad was coming to see him play. He wiped his nose on his shirtsleeve and backed away.

"I'll get there as soon as I can. Hit a good one for me."

****

Time crawled by like a centipede that had lost ninety-nine of its hundred legs. "My dad's coming to my game today," he told his pal Johnny as they rode their bikes down the dirt road on the farm where Johnny lived.

"Really? How did that happen?"

"He said his boss was letting him off early. I sure hope I don't mess up in front of him."

Johnny slowed down and smiled at his friend. "You don't have to worry 'bout that. You're the best player we got."

Wayne jerked his head sideways. Johnny had never said that before. Neither had anyone else. "You think so?"

"Sure. We always win when you're in the game."

"Then why does Mr. Daniel take me out?"

"You know why. It's 'cuz he plays everybody. He takes you out when we're ahead. Then he lets the others play."

Wayne thought for a moment. "Hope he leaves me in 'til my father shows up."

"Yeah, I hope he's not too late to see you play."

****

The baseball diamond was a flat, open field in rural Spotsylvania. Separating it from Mullen's Garage, a local car repair shop, were a chain link fence and a few oak trees. Most of the players lived on dairy farms, and their dads wanted them milking cows rather than playing ball. In spite of this, at least twenty-five or thirty eager boys usually showed up to play. Their parents knew Warwick Daniel was a dedicated church member, who had spent his only vacation working with boys in Vacation Bible School. He would be a good influence on their sons.

With peals of laughter and radiant faces they streamed into the makeshift diamond, trading their chores for a bat and ball. After Coach Daniel and another church member divided them up, there would be between ten and fifteen players on each team. Wayne almost always played for Coach Daniel.

By the sixth inning, the score was ten to five in favor of Daniel's team. Wayne had grown tired of watching for his dad to appear. He knew his coach would be putting the subs in soon. Even if his father showed up, he might not get to see him play.

Wayne walked up to bat, determined not to let disappointment affect his play. The pitch was right up the middle and he swung with all his might. The ball rocketed toward centerfield over the heads of all the fielders, hit the chain link fence that backed up the outfield, and bounced high into the air. By the time the centerfielder scooped it up, Wayne was heading home safe. The folks on the sideline were cheering and clapping. But the sweetness of his accomplishment soon faded and left bitterness in its place. His father wasn't there to see it.

Seconds after Wayne's teammates pounced on him to celebrate his home run, his father arrived. The next batter struck out, and the Daniel team headed to the field without Wayne. He watched his dad put his hand over his eyes to shield them from the bright sun as he combed the field for his boy. Then an angry scowl spread across his face as he spotted Wayne sitting on the ground.

He saw his dad march straight to Coach Daniel. "Why isn't my boy out there?"

"Why hello, Harry. You just missed your son's home run. He really creamed it."

Wayne held his breath as the frown sank deeper into his dad's face. "This is the first time I've been able to get off from my job, and I want to see him play. Why isn't he in the game?"

Wayne winced and hid his face in his hands. His cheeks burned as he waited for his coach to speak.

Coach Daniel stood up and looked straight into his father's eyes. His voice was calm and steady as he spoke. "This is Little League. I have almost thirty boys who have practiced hard and need to have some playing time. Getting in the game is their reward for hard work. That means your son has to come out to give the others a chance. I know you're disappointed, but I can't let any of them down."

Wayne's eyes were on his dad as he waved his hands in disgust, wheeled around, and looked down at his son. "Cm'on, boy. You might as well leave, too."

Red-faced, Wayne obeyed and trudged behind his father.

I pick up the receiver and shut off the speaker on my phone. Wayne's voice is somber and sad. "That was the only time I remember being embarrassed by my father. Your dad was so even-handed and fair-minded. He was a role model for me. I remember he was superintendent of Sunday School when I came to Salem Church. I was impressed at how well he handled that job. He was a great leader and was always interested in developing young people. I still have the birdhouse I built in his class in Vacation Bible School."

I tear up. "There's so much I've learned about my father since I've been writing this book. Thank you for calling. I'm so grateful that you've shared this with me."

ABOUT THE AUTHORS

David Black (*Skyline 2019* poetry judge; "As We Study an Old Photograph" and "All Hallows Eve," poetry), a retired English teacher and minister, is a former poetry editor of the *English Journal* and a frequent contributor of poems, essays, articles, and reviews to small magazines and academic journals, especially in the Appalachian region. He is the author of four books: *Some Task, Long Forgotten and Other Poems*, *The Clown in the Tent*, *Shortcomings: Around the Grounds & Corner*, and *Aspects of a Crosscut Saw*.

Stephen Bush (*Skyline* publisher; *Skyline 2019* nonfiction judge; "Winter, What Is It Like?" nonfiction), born in Singapore and an Australian citizen, now lives in southern Europe. He is the publisher for Cyberworld Publishing, is volume editor for the annual *The Good Life in Galicia* anthology; the author of the novel *My Sister's Funeral*; short story writer; and author of dog care and grooming manuals. He has run workshops on dog grooming, served as an Australian dog show judge, and raised Chinese Cresteds. Prior to moving to Europe, he lived on the east coast of Australia and for some years in Darwin. He has traveled extensively in northern Australia, where he worked as an accountant. Since arriving in Spain, he has restored several village houses for holiday letting and resurrected a small abandoned vineyard.

Carol G. Cutler ("From His Father's Arms: Sharim's Story," fiction; "Christmas Letter to My Sister," poetry) writes fiction, nonfiction, and poetry. She participates in several writing groups in the Charlottesville area, including a critique group of the Blue Ridge Writers. Her publications include clinical research in psychiatric nursing (1998), a contributing chapter in Theonomy and Autonomy (1985) on the relation of health care and theology, stories and poems in *Skyline 2017* and *2018* and in the Centennial Anthology of the Virginia Writers Club 2018. She has two sons and a daughter and four grandchildren.

P. A. Duncan ("A Visit from Grandfather Frost" and "Lull Them into a Sense of Complacency," fiction) is a retired bureaucrat but one with an overactive imagination—or so she's been told since she wrote her first stories using her weekly spelling words list. She graduated from Madison College (now James Madison University) with degrees in history and political science. Politics and history always find their way into her writing. Her fiction has appeared in numerous literary journals and anthologies and has won or placed in numerous contests. She is particularly proud of her short story, "Reset," which won the Virginia Writers Club 2016 Golden Nib Award for Best Fiction. Her debut novel, *A War of Deception*, received the New Apple Literary Award for Excellence in Independent Publishing as a Featured Selection in Historical Fiction. She is president emeritus of the Virginia Writers Club, one of the oldest writers' groups in the country. She lives and writes in the beautiful Shenandoah Valley of Virginia, where she also cheers on the New York Yankees, watches NASCAR, and spoils grandchildren.

Sarah Collins Honenberger (*Skyline 2019* fiction judge). Sarah's novel, *Catcher, Caught*, is a Pen/Faulkner Foundation selection in its Writers in Schools program. Audio, German, and Korean editions have been released. With numerous short fiction awards and a fellowship from the Virginia Creative Arts Center, she appears regularly on literary panels and at book festivals. Her other novels include *Minding Henry Lewis* (2014), *Waltzing Cowboys* (2009), and *White Lies: A Tale of Babies, Vaccines and Deception* (2006).

Gary D. Kessler (*Skyline* executive editor; "Shared Oreos," fiction; "A Monterey Christmas," nonfiction) is a former CIA analyst, news agency managing editor, diplomat, newspaper columnist, theater critic, movie consultant, book editor, and publishing consultant. His published works include the short story collections *On the Downtown Mall* and *Shadow of the Blue Ridge*; volume editor for the two-volume *WritersNet Anthology of Prose and Poetry* and the four-volume *Blue Ridge Anthology*; coauthor of a publishing reference, *Finding Go! Matching Questions and Resources in Getting Published* and of a Bible study, *(Re)Tell Me the Stories*; author of a mystery novel, *What the Spider Saw*; and author of the memory book *Of Me I Muse*. He has won or placed in multiple Virginia Writers Club annual contests and three times in the UVa Art Museum's Writer's Eye prose contest and took third place in the

John Gresham—judged *The HooK* short story contest in 2011. His poetry has appeared in the *Piedmont Virginian*. He also writes pen name mystery novellas and novels.

Gerry Kruger ("Coach Daniel," nonfiction), a native Virginian, moved in 1979 from Richmond to the Charlottesville area. She taught English for twenty-seven years at Charlottesville High School. Since 2004 she has participated as a judge in the Writer's Eye contest, sponsored by the University of Virginia's Fralin Museum of Art. As an essayist on National Public Radio, she detailed the adventures of a lame Canada goose that arrived at her pond on foot in 2000 and stayed with her for nine years. Her first book, *On Kruger Pond: Charlie's Story*, chronicles her unique relationship with this goose and his struggles and triumphs. Her second book, *Two of Us: A Father-Daughter Memoir*, has recently been published. Gerry visited her father every week in Fredericksburg in the last two years of his life and worked with him on the book. He died in February of 2018 at age ninety-eight and had read drafts of all the chapters. "Coach Daniel" is a chapter from this book.

Susan M. Lanterman ("Taking the Plunge," nonfiction) writes human-interest stories for the "Commentary" section of Charlottesville's *The Daily Progress* newspaper; is writing a collection of short stories entitled, "Good Night Already: Stories from a Reluctant Innkeeper," based on her Charlottesville B&B; and has written a young adult novel, *Hasta Luego, Santa Claus*, which follows the antics of a teenager and his family of illegal immigrants.

BAMorris ("Solstice Song," poetry) lives with her husband in Central Virginia. She writes short stories, memoirs, essays, and poetry.

Deborah M. Prum ("A Christmas Story," fiction; "O Christmas Tree" and "Dear Santa," nonfiction) is the author of *Fatty in the Back Seat* (a young adult novel), *First Kiss and Other Cautionary Tales* (an audiobook collection of humorous essays that first aired on NPR-member stations), *Czars and Czarinas* (an anecdotal and interactive history in iBook format) and *Rats, Bulls and Flying Machines* (a print book about the Renaissance). Her award-winning short fiction has been published in many places, including *The Virginia Quarterly Review*, *The Blue Ridge Anthology*, *Across the Margin*, and *The Sweetbay Review*. Her humorous essays appear in many places, including the *Washington Post* and Charlottesville's *Daily Progress*, and air on NPR-member stations. Her work can be seen at www.deborahprum.com.

Elizabeth Doyle Solomon ("Mama's Last Christmas, 1953" and "New Orleans Christmas, 1947," fiction; "A Christmas Morning Memory," "My First White Christmas," "A Christmas Reckoning," and "The Christmas Story," poetry), a New Orleans native and retired teacher, began writing at age eleven and publishing at age thirteen. Now in her seventies, she reckons her poems total over 60,000. Elizabeth has published two poetry collections, *Season*s and *The Steering Wheel Poems*, written newspaper columns, and founded the *Central Virginia Leader* newspaper. Her recent awards for both poetry and prose have come from the Poetry Society of Virginia, the Blue Ridge Writers, and the *Skyline* anthology. Until recently, Elizabeth led the Blue Ridge poets' critique group in her home, every Friday, for fourteen years. She is working on her third book, a collection of poems and short stories, *Journey West and Everywhere*.

Olivia Stowe (*Skyline* volume editor; "The Italian Crèche" and "Time for Grace," fiction) lives and writes in Central Virginia. Stowe's specialty is cozy mystery novellas, which include a thus-far eleven-volume series of Charlotte Diamond mysteries, the most recent of which is *Slave to the Past*. The Christmas season short stories, "Cassandra's Last Spotlight," "Blessedly Cursed Christmas," and "Jesus Speaks Galician" add to this series. She also is the author of the inspirational Savannah novella series. Stowe's standalone mysteries include *Fiddler's Rest*, *Restoration of the Castle*, and *Final Flight*. Her inspirational Christmas short story collections are available in the *Spirit of Christmas* and *Christmas Seconds* anthologies. This is the sixth annual volume of *Skyline* she has volume edited in conjunction with Cyberworld Publishing.

Erin Newton Wells ("A Time Coming Toward," fiction; "Recipe for Louisiana Thanksgiving," "A Few December Traditions," "Janus Face at Year's End," "A Litany for All Souls' Day," "Wheatfield with Crows," "A Chinese Birdcage," "Drink and Be Whole Again," "The Wasting Hydrangea," "Nevertheless Isabella Gibbons Reads," "As it Curves Beyond Memphis," "My Grandparents' House," and "Sliding from the Edge of the World," poetry; "Groundhog, Candle, Emily," nonfiction) has a background in visual arts and writing, working mainly with poetry. Her studies at the Universities of Texas and Arizona concentrated on creative writing and early Germanic and Celtic languages. A native of southeast Texas, she now lives in Virginia, where she developed and taught an extensive curriculum of studio art in a private school. Her poetry appears in such journals as *Spillway*, *A Sow's Ear*, *The MacGuffin*, and *Valley Voices*, and she has won many awards for her work, among them an Academy of American Poets University Prize.

~

Skyline 2018

The fifth collection of works by Central Virginia Writers

Skyline 2017

The fourth collection of works by Central Virginia Writers

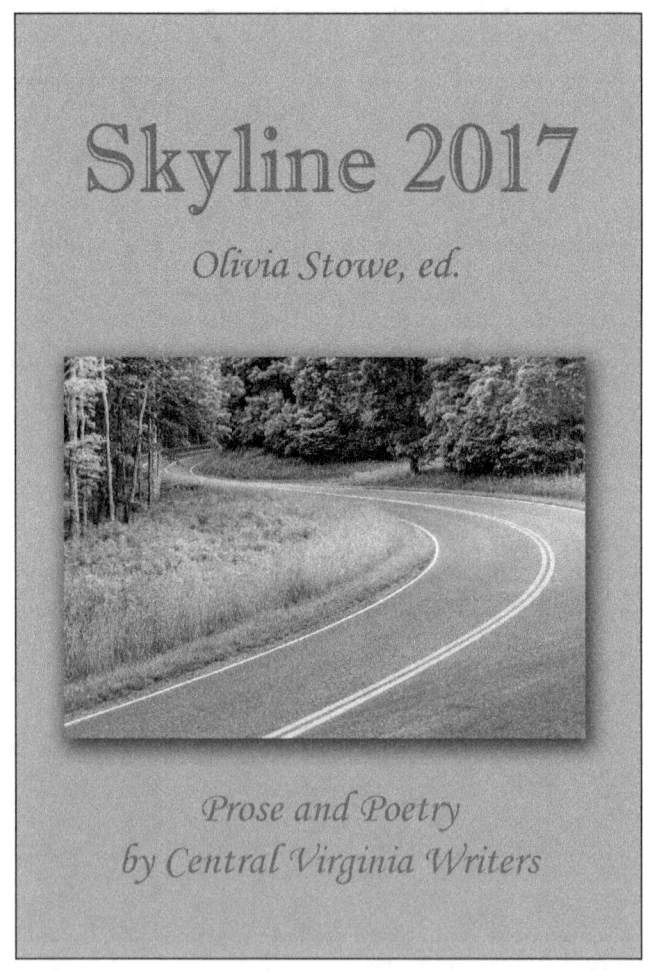

Skyline 2016

The third collection of works by Central Virginia Writers.

Skyline 2015

The second collection of works by Central Virginia Writers.

Skyline 2014

The first collection of works by Central Virginia Writers.

www.ingramcontent.com/pod-product-compliance
Lightning Source LLC
Chambersburg PA
CBHW061213170626
46809CB00003B/1343